# I.M.A.G.I.N.E. PEACE NOW

The Innovative Merger of Art and Guns to Inspire New Expressions of Peace Now

Published by
Boris Bally
Bally Humanufactured, LLC
789 Atwells Avenue
Providence, RI 02909
www.borisbally.com
peace@borisbally.com

First Printing, 2016
ISBN 978-0-692-80506-0
Library of Congress Control Number 2016918800

Essays edited by Monica Moses
Design and layout by Erin McManus Design, www.erinmcmanus.net
Type set in Freight Sans, Museo Sans & Raleway
Photos by Aaron and Lynn Usher, www.aaronusher.com, or courtesy of the artist unless otherwise noted.

Printed by J.S. McCarthy Printers
Augusta, Maine

Every reasonable attempt has been made to identify copyright holders. Any omissions or errors will be corrected in subsequent editions.

**Front cover:** *Bird of Prey* **by Marilyn da Silva**
Photo by M. Lee Fatherree, Oakland, CA

**This book was printed to coincide with the exhibition I.M.A.G.I.N.E. Peace Now**

**Wellington B. Gray Gallery
East Carolina University**
Greenville, NC
November 21, 2016 - January 16, 2017

**Society of Arts and Crafts**
Boston, MA
February 27 - June 10, 2017

The **I**nnovative **M**erger of **A**rt & **G**uns to **I**nspire **N**ew **E**xpressions. The I.M.A.G.I.N.E. PEACE NOW Exhibition, is a call to arms, hearts and hands intended especially for contemporary craft artists. Included work responds to, and initiates conversations regarding the gun violence prevalent in American culture today.

# CONTENTS

# FOREWORD

**Michael McMillan**

Associate Curator

Fuller Craft Museum

"...the end goal of "I.M.A.G.I.N.E. Peace Now" is not only to advance common sense firearm policies, but also, for the promotion of peace."

American society has prospered through a shared belief in hard work, the potential for upward mobility, and a deep-seated philosophical and emotional commitment to the core principle of personal liberty. However, events in the country today demonstrate that societal peace and personal safety are not inevitable byproducts of a commitment to freedom. In reality, the country struggles to accommodate peaceful discourse with regard to the spectrum of moral, social, and political perspectives competing against one another in American society. As a result, citizens often voice their contentions and fulfill personal agendas through the callous brutalization of their neighbors and authorities.

The most notable manifestation of the assault on personal safety has been the epidemic of gun violence. "I.M.A.G.I.N.E. Peace Now" is a timely place marker to reflect on this challenging state of affairs, as the metalsmithing community has rallied to push back the darkness precipitated in American society by pervasive violence and the wanton disregard for human life. That said, the end goal of "I.M.A.G.I.N.E. Peace Now" is not only to advance common sense firearm policies, but also, for the promotion of peace.

The moving content of this ambitious project emerged from the creative flames lit by the 1996 exhibition "Guns in the Hands of Artists." Organized at Positive Space Gallery in New Orleans by artist Brian Borello and gallery owner Jonathan Ferrara, the show featured artists who ingeniously reworked decommissioned street weapons (attained through a city of New Orleans buy-back program), to respond to the savagery carried out with guns in the mid-1990s.

News of their artistic accomplishments was documented by the media and ultimately highlighted in the New York Times. The NYT article came to the attention of trauma surgeon Matthew Masiello, S.W.A.T. Commander Lieutenant Phil Dacey, and attorney (now judge) Derwin Rushing. Dacey was the head of the guns buy-back program for the city of Pittsburgh, while Rushing's wife Darlene was the head of educational programming at the Pittsburgh Center for the Arts, where a metalsmith named Boris Bally had been a former instructor. With this web of connections in place, these three individuals moved forward with Bally in an endeavor meant to echo the success of "Guns in the Hands of Artists."

Through the Pittsburgh Metals Society, the Carnegie Museum of Art, and the enthusiastic support of others, the exhibition "Artists of a Different Caliber" opened at Carnegie Mellon University's Hewlett Gallery in 1997. The organizing and jurying committees were composed of an influential mix of artists and curatorial figures in the crafts and decorative arts. In 1998, this showcase of accomplished technical and conceptual metalsmithing would also make its way to the Charles A. Wustum Museum of Fine Arts in Racine, Wisconsin.

Tragically, the gun violence situation in America has only escalated since these exhibitions. The killing of students at Virginia Tech and Sandy Hook Elementary School, police-related shootings in Missouri, Minnesota, and Louisiana, and group-targeted killings in Orlando and Charleston have demonstrated that gun violence is a reality for individuals of every skin color, sexuality, religion, and socio-economic status. Boris Bally has recognized these heartbreaking circumstances, and "I.M.A.G.I.N.E. Peace Now" is his grand response. It will both challenge and entice viewers at East Carolina University and the Society of Arts and Crafts in Boston. It is fitting that the updated conversations encapsulated in "I.M.A.G.I.N.E. Peace Now" are again expressed through metalsmiths because they have the capacity to create these original objects of weaponry, as well as the skills to rework them for artistic purposes. Furthermore, this exhibition is pertinent for a field that has seen emotionally charged narrative content exemplified in greater complexity over the last 20 years.

Recognizing both the social context and the development of the project, the artists, jurors, curators, and publication designer of "I.M.A.G.I.N.E. Peace Now" explored this imperative topic with a balanced mix of sincerity, enthusiasm, and accountability. The hard work and collaboration that produced this exhibition were done in a manner reflective of the peaceful discourse the contributors hope to see adopted in American society to resolve this national problem.

# ESSAYS

## THE GUN AS MATERIAL

Reflecting on the process of rendering his iconic mobiles, American sculptor Alexander Calder once said, "A knowledge of and sympathy with the qualities of the materials used are essential to proper treatment."[1] Penned over seven decades ago, these words are eerily present in the works presented in "I.M.A.G.I.N.E. Peace Now." The artists selected for this exhibition know all too well the qualities, functions, and implications of guns as a material and a force in society, and their works demonstrate a deep sympathy with the pain guns continue to inflict on communities throughout the world.

Firearms are not inert media. They are neither paint nor canvas, neither paper nor pencil. As mechanisms, tools, and manufactured objects, they rely on a broad and twisted ecology of industries, legislators, lobbyists, government operatives, and marksmen. The artists included in the exhibition celebrate a contorted optimism – bending, warping, shattering, and transforming the form and, perhaps, the function of guns.

Nancy Fouts inverts a Spanish-made J. Cesar automatic pistol, replacing the pistol grip with a wooden pipe bowl and adding wood, feathers, and beads extending from the barrel to become her work "Peace Pipe". In "Checking the Cost of Gun Violence", Harriete Estel Berman implicates a revolver in a statement of accountability, becoming the handle of a check-writing machine processing the cost of mounting deaths from gun violence in America. Red ink leaks out, blood pools, amid a scatter of bullet casings. A direct gesture of challenge and resistance to the norms of guns in American life, Hoss Haley's sculpture "Pinch" presents a Colt Police Special rendered inert by a C-clamp pinching the barrel shut. Johanna Dahm and Johanna Stierlin's collaborative work "Hand in Hand" juxtaposes an inverted World War I- and II-era military pistol and a wax cast replica painted in skin tone and adorned with human hair. Using the technique of moulage – the art of creating mock injuries to train medical or military personnel – the work perhaps prompts the question of whether the gun has been injured by the application of humanity to its form.

This exhibition is indebted to the National Rifle Association, countless Senators and Representatives, companies such as Smith & Wesson, police departments across the country, the branches of the armed forces, and all those who take up firearms against their fellow humans. Without their tireless efforts and sacrifices to perpetuate the economics of gun manufacture and gun use, none of the artwork in this exhibition may have been possible.

[1]    Alexander Calder. 1943. A Propos of Measuring a Mobile, Unpublished Manuscript, Archives of American Art, Smithsonian Institution.

**Ian Alden Russell**

Curator

David Winton Bell Gallery

Brown University

"The artists selected for this exhibition know all too well the qualities, functions, and implications of guns as a material and a force in society, and their works demonstrate a deep sympathy with the pain guns continue to inflict on communities throughout the world."

# ESSAYS

**Jillian Moore**

Metals Artist

"Through the process of creative disarmament, these new objects can pursue multiple avenues of discourse – eroding, recontextualizing, and dismantling the totemic role of the gun in American culture. We have to start somewhere."

## UNMAKING

We think of metal as such an inviolable material. Along with "stone," we use "bronze" and "iron" to describe the technological advancement of civilizations. All of our worldly possessions made of metal will last long past our more organic bodily expiration date. We commemorate things that are fleeting, experiential, and sentimental with objects made of metal to try to tether them to the material world, making them somehow more tangible. Slip a great grandmother's ring on your finger, put an antique spoon in your mouth, hang an old horseshoe over your door, and you'll experience an existential grounding. That's why there's a potency to metalsmithing as an art practice. The cutting, forging, and casting of metal is so deeply pleasing because it imparts this power to the maker. There is deep satisfaction in the crunch of a sawblade through sheet metal and the grinding rhythm of the file – because metal does not take suggestions readily. It must be persuaded to lend its weight to your purpose, to bend or stretch or shine.

Because of this, I understand what is so seductive about the weight of a gun in the hand.

And because of this, I have a profound resentment for the employment of this material I love for an undeniably malignant purpose.

Guns are prescribed for the various cowboy afflictions of inferiority, braggadocio, and rage. We use the phrase "America's gun problem," as though it were something that just happened to us. But the dangerous conflation of liberty and weaponry is a congenital condition that dates back to our bloody birth as a nation.

How do we even begin to approach something so intractable?

Each maker and metalsmith in "I.M.A.G.I.N.E. Peace Now" was given a gun to take into their studio, to perform the symbolic ritual of neutering an implement of violence, to commit themselves to the act of "unmaking." They have persuaded these objects that were once guns to become other things. It is a first step in demystifying and disempowering them. Through the process of creative disarmament, these new objects can pursue multiple avenues of discourse – eroding, recontextualizing, and dismantling the totemic role of the gun in American culture. We have to start somewhere.

AWARDS

MARILYN da SILVA
*Bird of Prey*
Copper, gesso, colored pencil, deactivated gun
The feathers are etched copper. They were
made to fit the gun and soldered together. The
structure on the shadow is an anticlastic form.
5½" x 8" x 5¼"
Photo: M. Lee Fatherree, Oakland, CA

A raptor perches on the falconer's glove.

Its hood is removed and the prey is in sight.

Like a speeding bullet it reaches its mark,

Striking the target in a blink of an eye.

My piece weighs the metal of one handgun against 12,942 wild perennial lupine seeds. 12,942 because that was the number of people killed with guns in the United States in 2015.[1] I knew it was important for me to count each and every seed in the making of this work, but I didn't realize how difficult and revealing it would be until I began. At first, noticing the nuance in color and size, I thought about each seed representing an individual. As the number grew the thought of losing so much life and potential was overwhelming. But the most disturbing moment came after hours of counting, when I could no longer hold the sadness of so many deaths. I became aware that I was doing nothing more than moving seeds into piles 5, 10, 15, 20, 25...100...1,000. I wish that everyone who has a voice in the gun control debate would be required to count, one by one, the lives taken each year. Because it is unacceptable for us to become numb to what those numbers truly represent.

1       Mascia, Jennifer. "15 Statistics that Tell the Story of Gun Violence This Year." The Trace. https://www.thetrace.org/2015/12/gun-violence-stats-2015/ (accessed June 1, 2016)

**SECOND PLACE - SILVER**
*E. H. Schwab Award*

CAPPY COUNARD
*The Human Cost*
Metal from one handgun, 12,942 wild perennial lupine seeds, copper, maple
Forging, riveting, forming, carving
5" x 20" x 6"

THIRD PLACE - BRONZE
*Halstead Award*

LINDA SAVINEAU
*Peace Is Not A Game!*
Gun, titanium, steel,
plexiglass, coral
Hand sawing, fabrication
20" x 10" x 1"

After the terrorist attacks in Paris and Brussels (so close to home) I felt the need to express my feelings about religious intolerance and gun violence in one way or another. (As I'm writing this, there's news about another terrorist attack in Istanbul.) This project was the incentive I needed. A gun cut in two by the symbols of three major religions as well as the peace symbol, form a labyrinth. Three little red balls run freely in the labyrinth mocking the little plastic hand-held games we played with as kids. But peace is not a game! It is serious business.

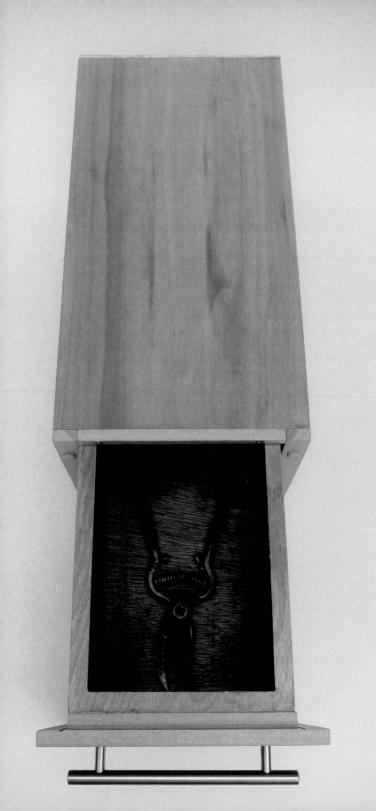

HONORABLE MENTION
*Halstead Award*

AARON KRAMER
*Weapons Into Shears*
Gun, poplar, walnut, brass, steel, delrin
Woodworking, welding, machining
7" x 8" x 16"

When the gun arrived I wanted to make it go away. I immediately disassembled it down to its most basic components in order to neuter its power. The purposefulness of its construction, the lack of ornamentation took me aback. There was an undeniable force that had to be reckoned with. I became obsessed with the trigger mechanism and the chamber. I had to shake off the allure. So I reassembled it and decide to make it disappear. I have always been fascinated with magic. Not necessarily the prestige of the presentation but with the inventiveness of the prop. There in lies the trick. Magic cabinets with false bottoms. Mirrors placed just so as to trick the eye. And full on mechanical automata that mimic real life and become another performer on the stage. I have little desire to be the conjuror with the wand but want to be the mechanic in the shadows. So I decided to make a magic cabinet that would transform the gun into a pair of pruning shears. A riff on a bible verse mixed with a little black magic. I consulted a book of "modern" magic from the 1890's that showed an illustration of a magic cabinet. These early boxes with false bottoms have been reproduced for years and can be purchased in magic shops today. But I wanted my trick to be automatic. Now you see it, now you don't. Repeat. So I started by making a drawer for the gun. And then another that fit perfectly around it yet was a little deeper. With very little planning I made a cabinet to house the two and then set about working on the mechanics. I struggled for days trying different ways of latching and unlatching the individual drawers. I was stymied and felt lost. Then late at night in the studio I turned on the radio to hear the sit-in at the House of Representatives demanding a vote on a gun control bill. I was inspired to press on and in an epiphany the idea of a ratcheting cam came to me. Just by chance my first iteration had 5 states of being. Gun, shear, shear, gun and gun. I liked the randomness of 5. Not gun, shear, repeat. So with much refinement I came up with a sequence that shows you the gun twice, then the shears, then the gun, then the shears and then the gun twice again. It is that unexpected quality that gives this trick its humanity. I hope it has the ability to transform minds and hearts. For when we can truly change our weapons into implements of good; tools that can be used to grow rather than kill; then we shall know true peace.

As a maker, investigating a variety of raw materials and pushing their intrinsic limitations to the point of beauty and/or disaster is continually enthralling. The firearm sent to me is layered with a rich history that is physically evident in the object's scratches, dings and cut off barrel. By exposing the firearm's guts and rendering the gun useless, the viewer can study the object's inner-workings without being afraid of its function.

**HONORABLE MENTION**
*Halstead Award*

**STACEY LEE WEBBER**
*Firearm Dissection #2*
Gun, resin, steel, mdf, acrylic
Resin pouring, sawing, welding
16" x 16" x 2"
Photo: Joseph Leroux

**HONORABLE MENTION**
*Doug White Award*

JOOST DURING
*Tête-à-tête*
Sterling silver, partial gun
Constructed cone hand-
hammered & formed
Pitcher: 10½" x 7" x 5"
Cups: 3¼" x 3" x 3"
Photo: Dean Powell

In my opinion guns make it far too easy to hurt or kill somebody before you have time to think about the consequences, or even have time to think why you are really upset. I have always believed in solving problems with conversation instead of violence and in taking a deep breath and thinking about things before you react.

Violence is almost never a solution and it usually destroys not only the life of the victim and their family but also the life of the perpetrator and their family. With my piece I am trying to make a statement, saying that it is better to sit down and share a cup of water or some other drink and talk about the issues you have with another person, to sit and take the time to really listen to each other and come to a non-violent solution.

As an artist I believe in the pursuit of an autonomous life and practice. However, when this pursuit of personal freedom begins to affect the lives of others, reality can come crashing down on philosophy. This is my struggle in trying to understand and have a position on gun control. The constant and horrific gun violence across the globe should challenge everyone's position on autonomy. This faceted intersection of freedom and restriction, violence and anger that we are all a part of, in our world, at this moment, is so powerfully imbued in the firearm as an object. It has been a challenging experience to work with a handgun for an art exhibition promoting peace. I believe I found a semblance of peace through transforming my handgun into a sling shot. A weapon becomes a toy. Aggression becomes childish and playful. What was once a confiscated firearm in an evidence locker is now rendered unrecognizable. Metal is strong, but can be accepting of change, under the right guidance and within the right circumstances. I believe the same can be said for the people in our world.

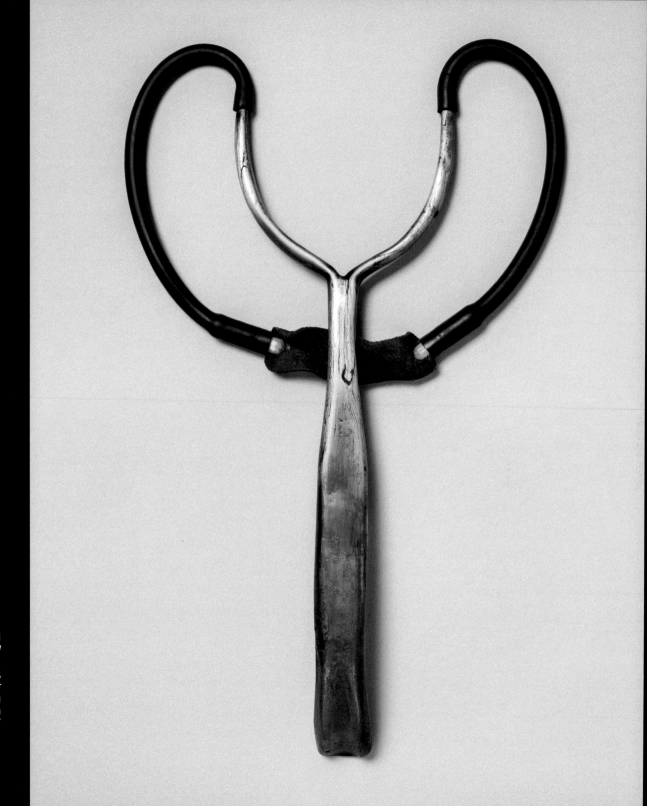

**HONORABLE MENTION**
*CRAFTHAUS Award*

**SANDRA ENTERLINE**
*Baby Bones*
*(In Memory of Sandy Hook)*
Handgun, paint, baby teeth, rodent bones
Fabrication, painting
4" x 6" x 1¼"
Photo: David Martinez

On December 14, 2012, a mentally unstable man fatally shot 20 children and six adult staff members at an elementary school in Connecticut. The handgun, often extolled as a symbol of masculinity and power, or representing a misguided sense of safety, is stripped of its industrial black sheen to reveal the true cost of gun ownership: its capacity to cause unfathomable grief. Mesmerizingly beautiful in its fragility, this handgun is enveloped in a skin of tiny bones, from femurs to vertebrae to baby teeth. In order to use this gun, one would have to literally break the tiny bones and feel the splinters digging into one's hand.

*Dedicated to Shyanne Charles, Joshua Yasay, Evan Rouse and Kamal Hercules, R.I.P*

The pieces of our youth tell many stories- stories and experiences that often make us who we are. Unfortunately, for many of us in North America and across the globe, those pieces also include firearms and gun violence, leaving our communities in pieces, shattered and torn.

Words cannot fully explain what this does to us mentally and emotionally so we hang our heads in sorrow and with hats over heavy hearts, we grieve as one. Our falling tears and blank stares speak a thousand words. Educating the youth on the value of human life is crucial.

KNOWLEDGE IS POWER, ARM YOURSELF

**HONORABLE MENTION**
*Kendall College of Art & Design Award*

ERIC PETERSEN & MARKO NEOFOTISTOS
*Pieces (of Youth)*
.25 cal Automatic glock, gold-plated brass,
lambskin, recycled skateboard wood & hardware,
acrylic, wool
Hand-cut/pierced, needlework
20" x 7½" x 5"
Photo: Matt Barnes

ARTIST WORK

ROBERT EBENDORF & ZACH LECHTENBERG
*Making Angels*
Mixed media: found materials and enamel
Hand crafted using wire cutting, enameling, and mixed media
12" x 6" x 1½"
Photo: Tara Locklear

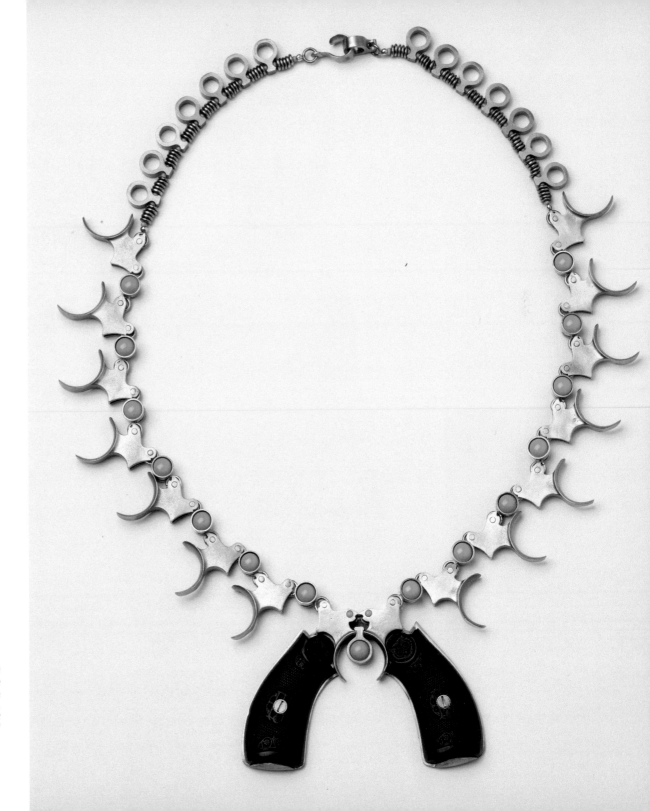

**LEEANN HERREID**
*Squash Blossom Necklace*
Brass, steel, silver, and turquoise
Casting, Soldering, filing, stone setting,
polishing, plating and a whole lot of ingenuity
14" x 10" x 1"

I live, work, and raise my son in Baltimore City, Maryland. Our city has one of the highest gun violence rates in the United States. Every day, someone is killed or wounded due to the simple fact that it is so easy to acquire a firearm here. To date, this year, we have already suffered 130 shooting deaths. However, I refuse to live in fear, to give in, or to give up. Despite the fact that I live in a war zone of violence, I love my city, my community, and my neighbors. We work together to support each other, to feel safe, and to look out for one another. That being said, every day I see deplorable living conditions, poverty, social injustice, and a lack of governmental and institutional support for our communities. This ignorance feeds violence, tears lives apart, and escalates our desperate cry for help.

Leaders and politicians who have not yet responded to our urgent cry for action on gun control legislation are responsible for turning a blind eye on our demands to stop the violence, to stop the killing, here, at home. How many more must go before we come together and stop this madness?

'Chatelaine for the Slain' is a Momento Mori, a tool of 'equipage' to aide in the remembrance of, and to honor every victim of gun violence, their families, and their loved ones. It is a wearable collection of keepsakes; a reminder that we must not forget any life that has been lost due to our country's failure to control gun availability to the hands of the unfit. It is a warning to all that no one is exempt from the reality of experiencing this kind of horror and loss, until we make change happen.

STOP THE VIOLENCE.
ONLY LOVE MATTERS.
IMAGINE PEACE NOW!

KIRSTEN WILLETT ROOK
*Momento Mori: Chatelaine for the Slain*
Disabled and dissected Hopkins & Allen safety Police 32 black powder break action revolver: circa 1904-16, fine silver fused and woven chain, sterling silver, mild steel, 18k gold, wood, vintage drawer pull, vintage soap dish, soap, vintage radiator steam vent, artist's son's baby tooth, vintage watch case, vintage folding magnifying glasses, optometrist's lenses, digital images.
Metalsmithing, assemblage
18" x 6" x 5"
Photo: Kyle Tata

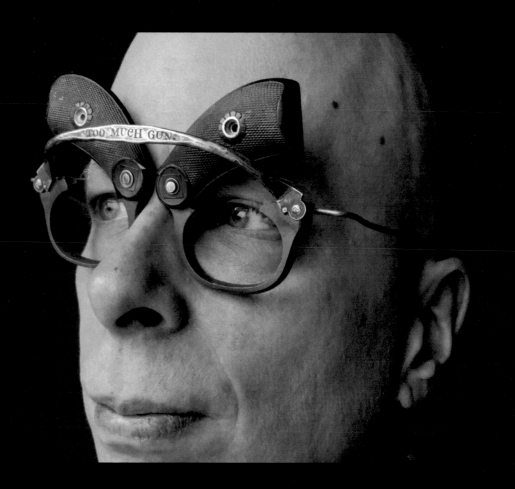

KEITH LO BUE
*Too Much Gun*
Revolver parts, brass, nickel
Cold-connected, etched, oxidized
3" x 5¾" x 8½"
Photo: Irena and Keith Lo Bue

**DAUVIT ALEXANDER - THE JUSTIFIED SINNER**
*Walk like a Man (Sex Crime)*
Gun; found, corroded iron, silver, cubic zirconia
Gun has been cut with a spark-erosion cutter; CAD-
designed elements 3D printed in wax and cast; hand-
formed; hand-set and polished
Size: Variable

Stamping out gun violence in the USA has experienced many false starts, or perhaps more optimistically, tentative beginnings. As we have learned, it will take a concerted effort from a united force. The weapon in this work has endured nine strikes of a six-hundred-pound drop hammer. At half its original width it has become practically a shadow, but as if mocking its imperfect destruction, it now grins from where it split a seam. The finished work shackles the gun to a steel chain, completing its metamorphosis from hand tool to body adornment. Strung like the albatross, guns continue to smile malevolently at us from their position of power, around our collective neck.

MELISSA CAMERON
*Resilience*
Gun, steel
Hot forging, assembly
7" x 7" x 2" on a 10' chain

**RANDALL CLEAVER**
*Butterfly*
Gun, gears, brass tube, metal
finial, wood peg, steel fly
wheel, clock
Dermal cut off wheel and
hack saw to split the gun in
half, metal lathe to turn brass
shaft collars and bushings.
Taps and dies for assembly.
19½" x 8½" x 12"

I set out to create a sculpture with a gun that would
be disarmed without altering the gun itself, somehow I
didn't want to have anything to do with it physically and
to present an alternative reality for it. I decided to make
a traditional Japanese shishi-odoshi fountain, thinking
I could hide the gun by making it fit in an ornamental
garden, by adding water in place of fire, and by
automating it to take away the human element. Shishi-
odoshi, when translated from the Japanese literally,
means "scare deer" and most often refers to a fountain
that startles animals away from ornamental plantings
or gardens, but is soothing and enjoyed by people.
This fountain too draws me in, but the knocking, the
mock-firing and loading over and over brings me back
to my senses, a reminder that our work is not complete.
Guns pose a threat to the safety of our families and
communities and we must remain diligent in our efforts
towards empathy, understanding and education to truly
disarm gun-culture and practice peace.

- HOWIE SNEIDER

**HOWIE SNEIDER**
*Shishi-odoshi - the Bell of Peace*
Forged steel, brass bullets,
decommissioned hand gun
Forging, welding, fabrication
11" x 12" x 7"

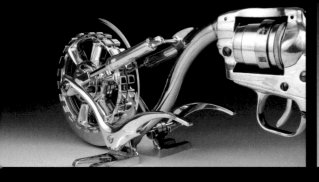

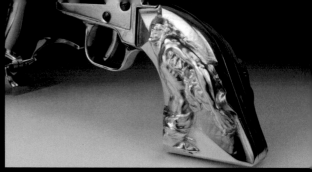
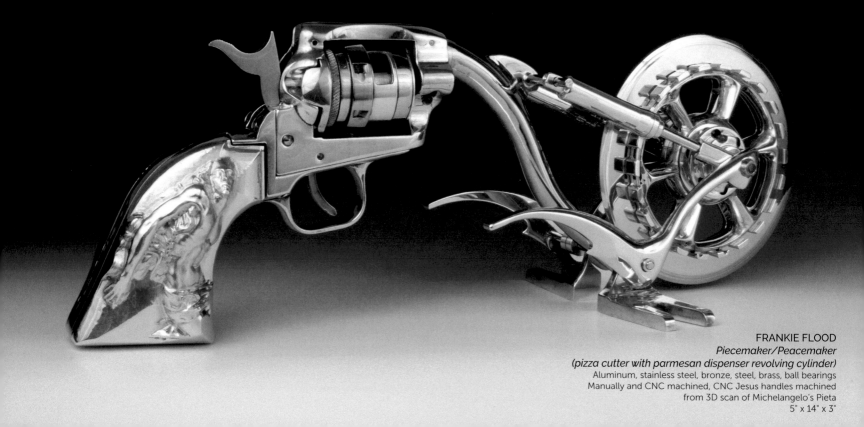

FRANKIE FLOOD
*Piecemaker/Peacemaker*
*(pizza cutter with parmesan dispenser revolving cylinder)*
Aluminum, stainless steel, bronze, steel, brass, ball bearings
Manually and CNC machined, CNC Jesus handles machined
from 3D scan of Michelangelo's Pieta
5" x 14" x 3"

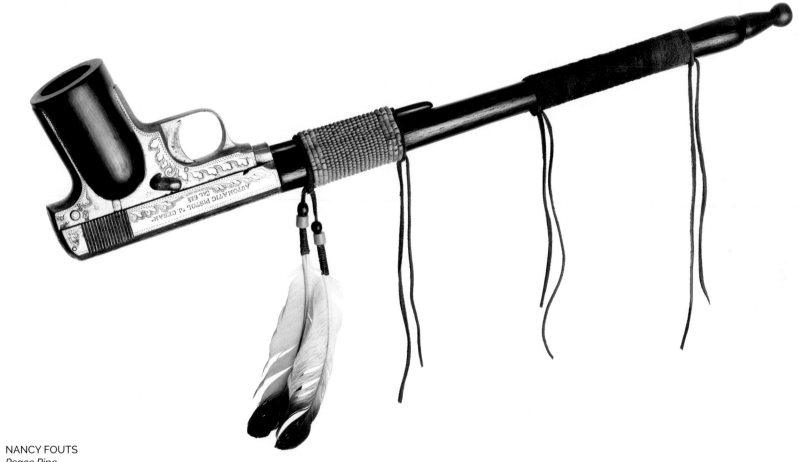

NANCY FOUTS
*Peace Pipe*
Gun, wood, feathers, leather, beads
combination of ideas and materials/objects
10" x 14" x 2½"
Photo: Dominic Lee

BILL DUROVCHIC
*Gunslinger's Tool*
Disabled revolver, disabled hand brace
Cut, grind, mill, turn on a lathe
12" x 6" x 2"

TIMOTHY LAZURE
*Ladle for Peace Punch*
Gun, steel, copper, leather
Hand molded leather, forged steel,
formed copper
3½" x 17" x 3¾"

ROB JACKSON
*Single Shot*
Muzzleloader, espresso machine, cups & saucers
Fabrication
11" x 16" x 9"
Photos: Aaron Usher (this page)
Rob Jackson (opposite page, top left)

This work transforms a single shot muzzleloader pistol into an implement for making a single shot of espresso. The Second Amendment was written when guns fired a single shot at a time. After each shot, the gunpowder had to be measured, poured into the barrel of the gun and carefully tamped down with the lead ball before re-firing. The same process is used for making a single shot of espresso: measuring the ground espresso and tamping it down into the holder before brewing. Both actions require approximately the same amount of time and are in stark contrast to automatic weapons of today.

<<<

>>>

JAN LONEY
*Tea for None*
Steel, silver
Fabricated and welded
construction, hydraulic die
formed tea infuser parts,
hand woven fine silver wire
on cylinder/infuser
16½" x 9¼" x 9¼"
Photos: Matt Dayak

CHARLES CROWLEY
*Hot Glue Gun*
Gun, mixed media
Transformation of purpose
9" x 12" x 1"

**RENEE ZETTLE-STERLING**
*We Mourn Our Loss*
Gun, ribbon, copper, brass, rubber
Cold connections, sewing
16" x 16" x 20"

This work is inspired by the ribbons worn by mourners during Abraham Lincoln's funeral. I wanted to draw parallels between the collective mourning for Lincoln and our collective mourning for all those who have been lost to gun violence. Our contemporary society does not encourage expression of collective mourning, as it did for Lincoln, but I believe this is an important perspective and one that I want viewers to contemplate.

The deconstruction of the gun into many parts allows us to reflect on how simple and innocuous parts can come together to create an object loaded with myriad associations, the potential for incredible harm, and boundless pain. Most Lincoln mourning ribbons had his image included, furthering people's ability to empathize and to acknowledge the collective loss to society. In my ribbons, I also wanted to replace his image with a part of the gun, allowing the viewer to meditate on the scourge and epidemic of gun violence.

**HARRIETE ESTEL BERMAN**
*Checking the Cost of Gun Violence*
Check writing machine, gun, 89 shells from bullets,
recycled tin, paint, silver, screws
Hydraulic matrix die form for fabricating new gun
handle grip from recycled tin cans, hollowware
forming of recycled tin for pool of blood, riveting
for lettering assembly, grinding and polishing to
retrofit gun to handle, paint for blood on check
writing machine, tap & die
8" x 15½" x 16"
Photo: Philip Cohen

KEN BOVA
*An Archaeology of Politics*
Sterling, 23k gold leaf, vitreous enamel on copper, gun barrel,
bones, U.S. currency, wood, acrylic
Fabrication, enamiling
3" x 2½" x ¼"
Photos: Aaron Usher (left), Ken Bova (right)

APRIL WOOD
*Ka-Bloom*
Steel, silver
Hand sawing, welding, soldering
8" x 10" x 9"
Photo: Joseph Hyde

I live in Baltimore, Maryland, and although I have not been a victim of gun violence myself, I see on a daily basis the effects of a city besieged, where more than 300 people were killed by guns in 2015. In the time since this call opened, we as a nation have witnessed the deadliest mass shooting incident to date. I chose to approach the challenge of the exhibition by subverting the inherent violence of the object through beauty and subtle humor. My work often utilizes feminine and botanical imagery to challenge the masculine materials I work with. I hand-pierce steel in elaborate lace patterns, that act as funnels, filters, or growths off of the body. In Ka-Bloom, steel lace emerges from the barrel of the gun, unfurling and folding in a way that mimics the blooming of a flower. The steel lace eliminates the function of the gun, while also toying with the metaphor of male virility as sometimes symbolized by guns. Additionally, the imagery (and title) references the bang flag often used for comic relief in cartoons, as well as the iconic image from the Vietnam War era of a protestor putting a flower in the barrel of a National Guard serviceman's gun.

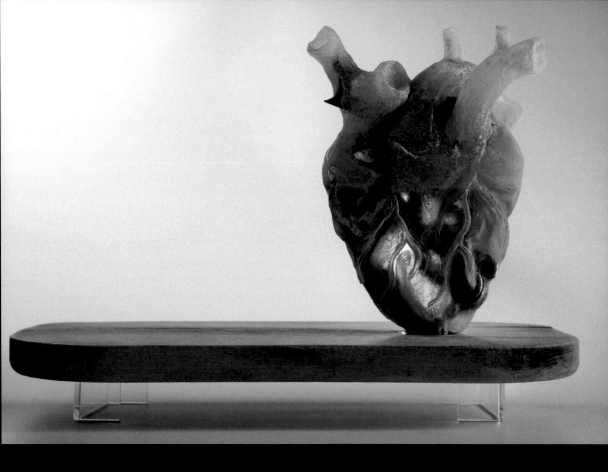

# MEL ALVES
*Black Tinted Heart*
Steel gun, resin, wood, acrylic
Dissected steel gun assembled into a heart shape, resin
casting and carved heart out of a sculpted colar heart
8" x 12" x 8"
Photo: Richard Bluecloud Castaneda

CHRISTINE CLARK
*Static*
Mild steel
Torch welded
10" x 8" x 16"
(hanging on 41" chain)
Photo: Stephen Funk

Suspended and encased in a cloud of static, an adorned gun reminds us that noise and voices are present while no one really hears. Beneath the interference is fear, the loss or gain of power, and blatant disrespect. This ingenious object, often beautifully designed, hovers in a prickly nest of intangible opinions, rarely making good sense of its presence.

NASH QUINN
*Gun Logic*
Armsco .22lr revolver, gold-plated
silver, paint
Drilled, etched, fabricated, painted
4" x 7" x 2"

*Made in USA*

I chose to transform this weapon by its own means ' making holes. A gun's purpose is to make holes in a thing and kill it, and I applied that methodology to the gun itself. My goal was to transform the weapon into a sublime and mysterious relic of its previous capacity for death -- a bone-like, decaying, memento that serves as a convenient visualization of the porous and rotten rhetoric surrounding "gun logic" in the United States.

SUE AMENDOLARA
*Opportunity for Grace*
Sterling silver, holly, 22k/SS mokume gane, gun parts
Formed, forged, fabricated & carved wood
4" x 4" x 3¼"
Photo: Robert Thomas Mullen

At nineteen years old, Sonya Arrington's son, Steve, was the victim of a shooting death in Erie, PA and in response to her grief, she founded Mothers Against Teen Violence, an organization to reduce youth and gun violence. I have seen this type of reaction to violence throughout history and am amazed at the courage and strength it must take to turn a personal tragedy into an 'Opportunity for Grace.' This piece is meant to honor those selfless actions of these brave individuals who overturned their grief and anger to create something hopeful for others in need.

I used imagery of rice patties and the new sprouts of the rice plant using precious materials and transforming parts of the gun I was given. Fields of rice patties are peaceful and contemplative to me and I referenced the idea of growth as a symbol of hope and change.

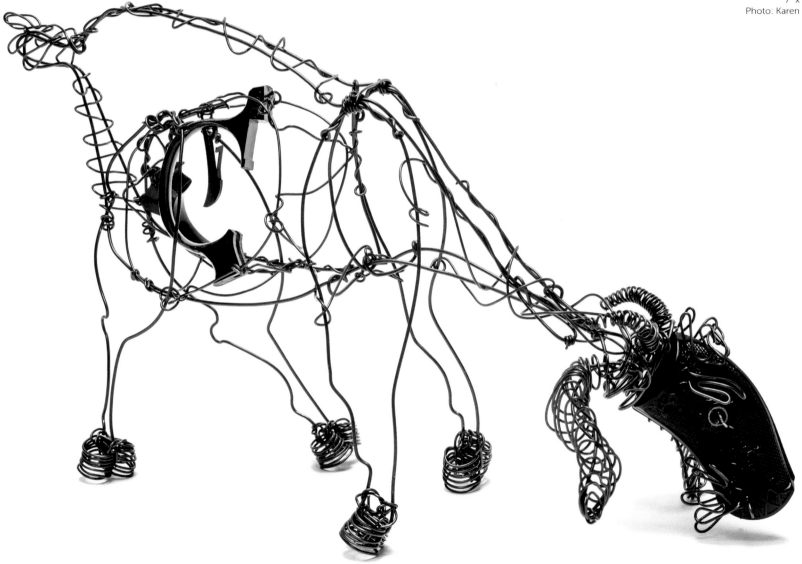

THEA ERNEST
*Trigger Happy*
Revolver parts, steel wire
Hand manipulated
7" x 12" x 4"
Photo: Karen Philippi

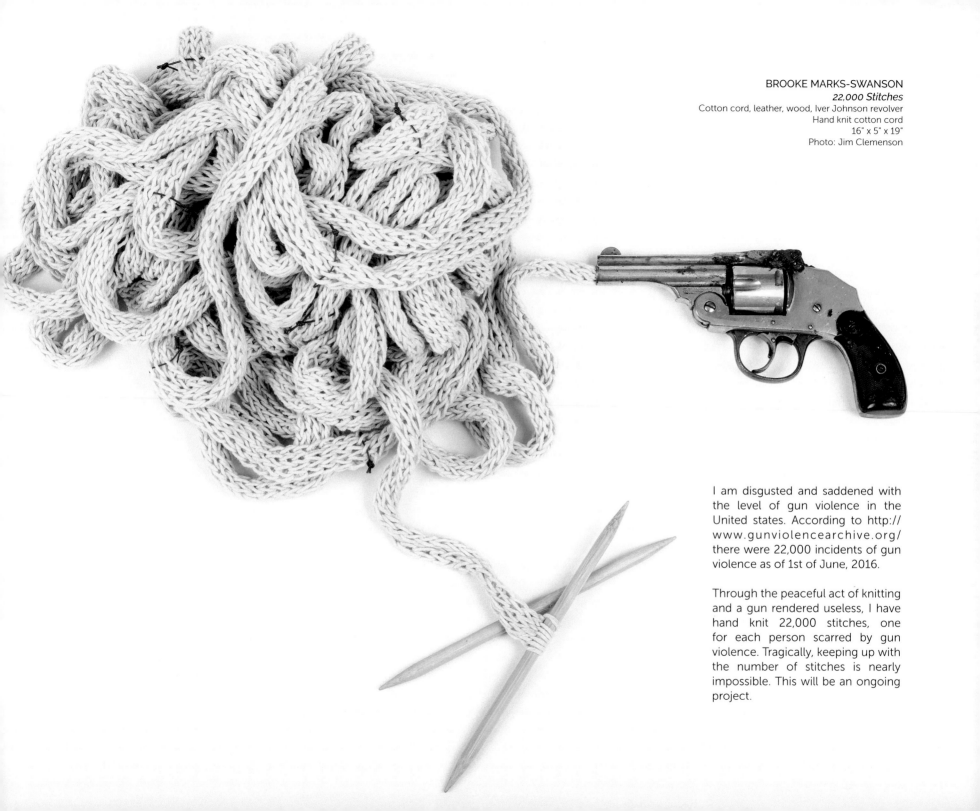

BROOKE MARKS-SWANSON
*22,000 Stitches*
Cotton cord, leather, wood, Iver Johnson revolver
Hand knit cotton cord
16" x 5" x 19"
Photo: Jim Clemenson

I am disgusted and saddened with the level of gun violence in the United states. According to http://www.gunviolencearchive.org/ there were 22,000 incidents of gun violence as of 1st of June, 2016.

Through the peaceful act of knitting and a gun rendered useless, I have hand knit 22,000 stitches, one for each person scarred by gun violence. Tragically, keeping up with the number of stitches is nearly impossible. This will be an ongoing project.

SELIENA COYLE
*Between the Sights of the Sun*
Photographic print on aluminum
Photo documentation
10" x 12" x 2"

As a catholic child born at the onset of what is commonly known as the Troubles, guns were part and parcel of everyday life. British soldiers patrolled the streets wielding assault rifles and would often stop, kneel and take aim at some imaginary target. Police officers were equally well-armed. This was countered by the existence of covert operatives, namely the IRA, whom one did not readily encounter but who instilled equal if not more fear through reputation alone. I imagine they were also pretty well equipped but that is more speculation than knowledge.

To be involved was short-hand for actively participating in events that would generally come under the guise of the Troubles. None of my family were involved, well I say none, involvement need not require a gun.

A perverse reality right?....but it has to be said that I experienced a very safe, family-orientated upbringing until the day I became an unwilling participant in the Troubles. I have never really spoken about this event except to close friends as it does not comply with the norm and so cannot be easily explained. Suffice to say, members of the IRA entered my family home where I was the only occupant, and it being exam time, was enjoying a day's relief from school. They proceeded to create what can only be described as a hostage situation which involved being trussed up like an oven-ready turkey and interrogated for what seemed like hours. This is when I experienced my first and only encounter with the cold hard pressure of a gun being held to my knee. The long and short of it was an assumption that my dad was in the RUC (police force) which he wasn't and for which I assume they were going to assassinate him. Fortunately this did not happen.

When my parents eventually did arrive home, the innards of a burst beanbag declared something was amiss. They did not enter the house but instead startled a woman on her way to the local shop with screams of blue murder. I am not exactly sure how it all came to an end but it did. To this day memories of the subsequent weeks are a blur of sadness and realization of innocence lost.

So when Boris invited me to make a piece for this exhibition I speculated on multiple iterations. That was until the gun arrived, was unpacked and in hand. The reaction was visceral. I could see no way to repurpose this instrument designed to kill or maim. I could not detach from the notion of previous use. My immediate reaction was that of disposal. I didn't want it near me or in the same house that 30 years earlier had hosted its *Doppelgänger*.

Research led me to stories relating to the transportation of guns from the US to Ireland in support of paramilitary activity. An irony almost unbearable in the current political climate. The infamous Boston crime boss Whitey Bulger, obsessed with the IRA, would send arms shipments in the coffins of dead compatriots being transported back to the auld sod. These arms would sometimes be interred in remote areas of bogland for retrieval at a later date. This starkly contrasts with the retrieval of bodies, victims of sacrificial killings historical and contemporary from the landscape in which they had been deposited.

The gun will be buried at an undisclosed site in Ireland in the hope of non-discovery. If it is unearthed the detector will have clues to the source of a strange disabled tool as it will have assumed a new branding, that of the exhibition title Imagine Peace Now.

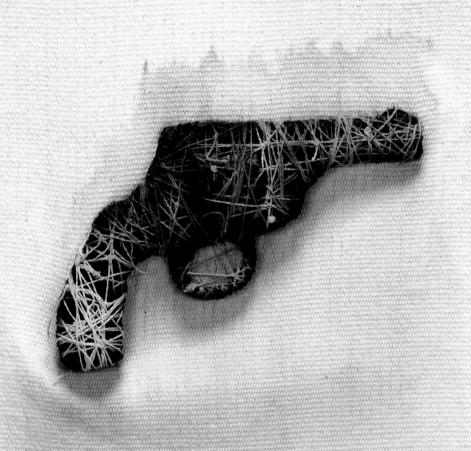

Unmendable: not capable of being mended. The foundation of this piece lies in the domestic, the soft, the safe. Hand woven cloth, stitching, and mending. These symbols of home have encased and surrounded the revolver. However the attempt to conceal has failed. The rust from the gun has stained the white cloth, while the weight of the revolver pulls and distorts the fabric. The rust runs down the cloth, shed tears for those lost.

IRENE LaVON WALKER
*Unmendable*
Hand woven cloth, revolver, thread
Weaving, stitching, rusting
19" x 15¼" x 1½"
Photo: Paul-David Rearick

KEITH BELLES WAX JEWELRY DESIGN STUDIO
*The Life Cycle of a Hand Gun*
Disabled hand gun, sterling silver, bronze, gold gilding
Distressed gun with vinegar and rain water, lost wax casting of
hand carved wax models. Polishing and patina finished metal.
7" x 4" x 1½"

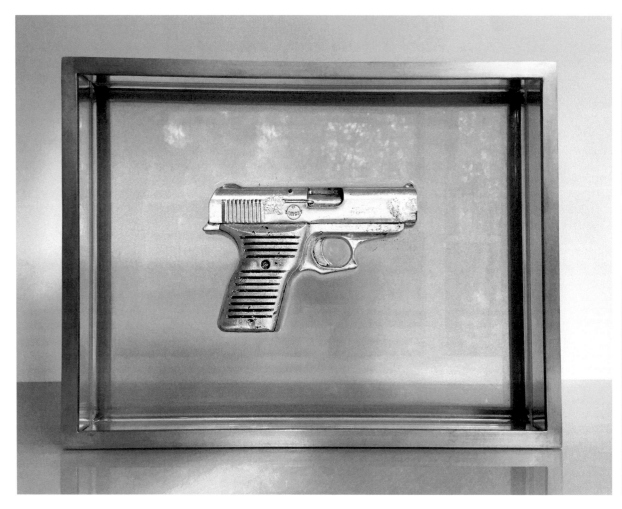

PETER DIEPENBROCK
*American Obsession*
Silicone bronze, epoxy resin, handgun, metal leaf, mirror
The gun was gilded. The bronze frame was fabricated and tig welded. The interior facing surfaces of the bronze frame
were then lined with mirror. The resin was poured in ⅛" layers, to fill half the box frame, and partially encase the gun.
10⅝" x 14" x 3"

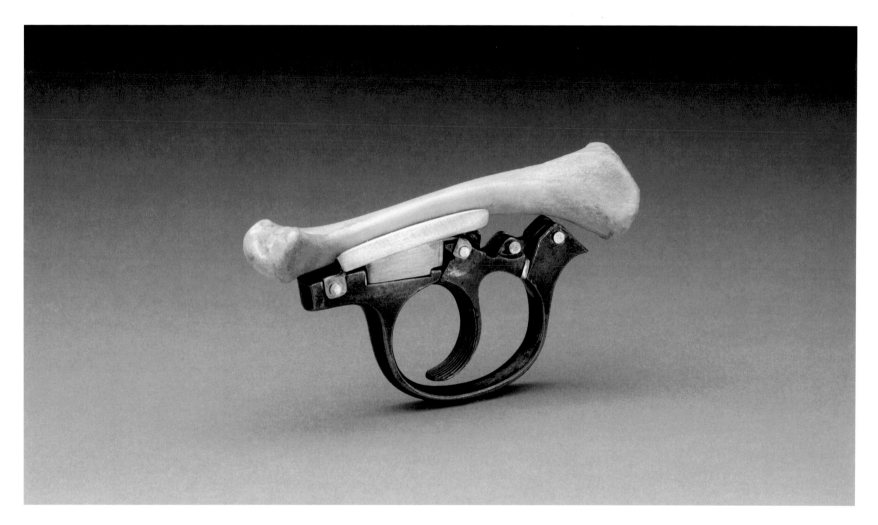

CLAIRE SANFORD
*13894*
Steel gun parts, sterling
silver, bone
Construction, cold joining
2" x 3" x ½"

**HOSS HALEY**
*Pinch*
Bessey C-Clamp, Colt Police Special 32-20 WCF
I used a hydraulic press to crush the barrel into the shape of the C-Clamp
4" x 6" x 12"
Photo: Steve Mann

The role of firearms in American history is vast and complicated. My personal views on gun control, however, are very simple. There are some weapons to which none of us should have access. And, there are some people who should not have access to any firearms. It was my intention to respond to this project with the same direct and uncomplicated approach.

ANDREW HAYES
*Window*
Steel and firearm
Steel fabrication
15" x 8" x 3"
Photo: Steve Mann

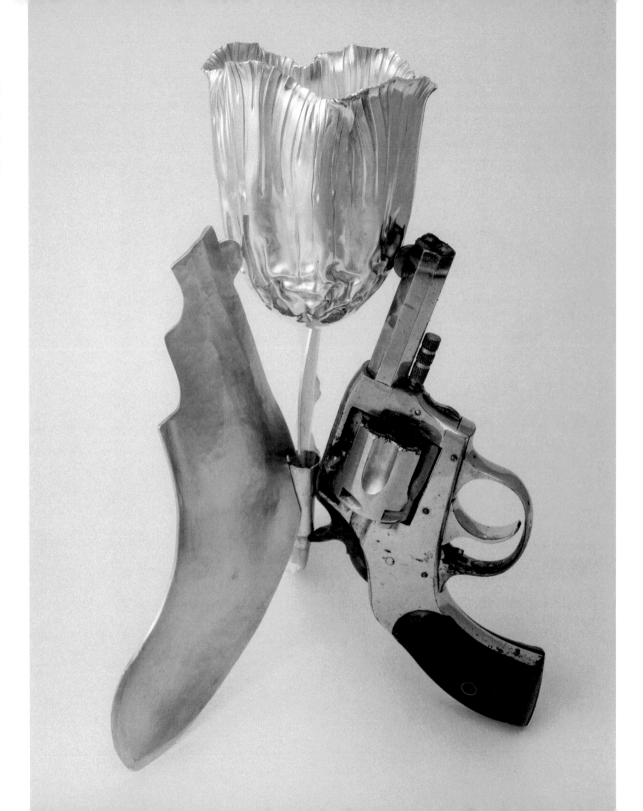

CYNTHIA EID
*Swords Into Plowshares*
Gun, bullet, nickel alloy,
argentium sterling silver
Fusing, hammer-forming,
hydraulic press embossing
and deep drawing, forging,
sawing, soldering
10" x 7" x 7"

ROBERT COOGAN
*A Dish Served Cold*
Found objects, gun, aluminum
plate, brass, copper, lead
Bullet fired through plate,
forming, assemblage, chisel
engraving, stamping
2" x 16" x 16"

DIANNE REILLY
*Kindergarten*
Brass, steel, wax, epoxy and gun
Fabrication, etching and casting wax
7" x 7" x 7¼"
Photo: Dean Powell

Children die each day because of the presence of guns in their environment. It is natural for a child to try to understand the world around them by looking, by touching and by exploring. Their brains are physiologically unable to make tangible connections between life and death.

This piece speaks about the countless children who have been killed by guns as well as our own apathy towards those small lives lost. As members of society we are culpable for each child that dies at the hand of a firearm. Theirs is not a choice but an effect of systemic neglect.

STEPHEN YUSKO
*Safe House*
Steel, glass, phenolic sheet
Forged, machined and fabricated
9" x 14¼" x 5"
Photo: Dan Morgan

DINDY REICH
*"186"*
Wood, copper, brass, maps, disabled gun, bullet casings, coated copper wires
Fabrication, wood construction, repousse and metal tooling
16" x 12" x 3½"

Adopted on December 15, 1791, The Second Amendment of the United States Constitution reads: "A well regulated Militia, being necessary to the security of a free State, the right of the people to keep and bear Arms, shall not be infringed." Throughout the history of the United States, there has been an ongoing debate about the intention of this Amendment and the rights of its citizens related to firearms. My piece, "Reliquary for the 2nd Amendment: 7 Pendants", is comprised of seven wearable pendants displayed together on a wall-mounted plate made of maps of the United States. Each pendant contains a different part of a disabled revolver encased in cast resin and housed in a ring made from a recycled book. The pattern on the back of each pendant is the "Lorem Ipsum" passage used traditionally as an empty text placeholder. All of the included text and maps are unreadable just as I believe the Second Amendment has become due to endless debate. Perhaps the wearing of the pendants will provoke fresh discussion about the impact of firearms on our daily lives.

JAMES THURMAN
*Reliquary for the 2nd Amendment: 7 Pendants*

For this exhibition the idea came to me via Iowa, Bill House File 2281, which made it legal for a toddler to own, possess, and handle a pistol, revolver, and ammunition.

To me it begged a question: what type of handgun would be the most appropriate gift for these toddlers to fill that last minute item for the stocking at Yule Time, or the perfect gift to be opened at a two-year-old's birthday while surrounded by his/her play date friends? The choices, as we all know, are endless and relatively inexpensive, and can be purchased in quantity in some States. I suggest a brassy, special 44 that will fit snugly holstered onto a diapered child as he/she makes his/her first attempt to go from a crawl to a standing walk. What could possibly go wrong?

STEPHEN F. SARACINO
*Iowa House Bill File #2281*
Brass, diaper made from flag
material, purple heart
Fabricated brass rod, sewn
diaper
16" x 10" x 8"
Photo: Bruce Fox

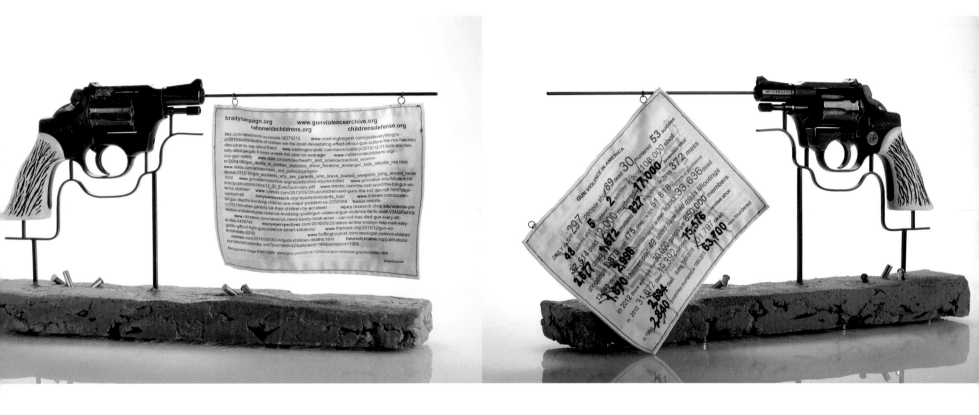

BIBA SCHUTZ
*Another Day*
22 revolver, painted brass, printed cotton fabric,
colored thread, cement, bullet shells
Constructed and painted metal armature, printed and
embroidered cotton flag, cast cement
9" x 16" x 3"
Photo: Ron Boszko

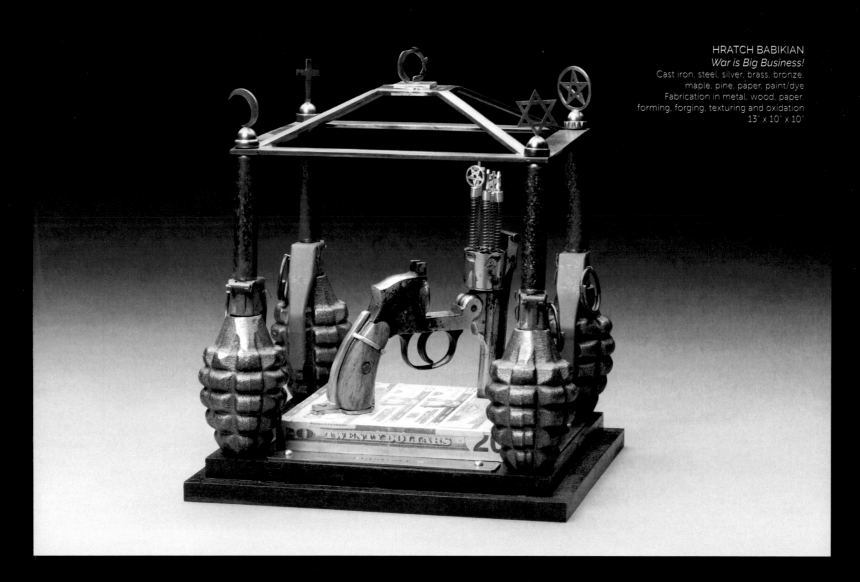

HRATCH BABIKIAN
*War is Big Business!*
Cast iron, steel, silver, brass, bronze,
maple, pine, paper, paint/dye
Fabrication in metal, wood, paper.
forming, forging, texturing and oxidation
13" x 10" x 10"

For Millennia, Humankind has gone to war over religion and we are still warring over differences of belief in religion. In my personal experience, there seems to be another facet to the disagreements: There is usually a group which exploits the differences of opinion and resulting violence by fulfilling the need for arms and profiting by selling, or servicing, the weaponry to either side. In our time, the gun manufacturers have now become just as powerful as the tobacco industry once was. Both industries are aware that what they produce is causing enormous, tragic loss of life. As long as the manufacturers, the owners, shareholders, C.E.O.'s of these companies are profiting from the sales of guns, the problem of gun violence in the USA will never be under control.

PIERRE CAVALAN
*Paris, Brussells, Orlando...*
Assembly including an egg shell
Mixed media
14¼" x 6¼" x 6¼"

71

**BILLIE JEAN THEIDE**
*"...shame and sorrow..."*
Iver Johnson Model
57 revolver, US
commemorative postage
stamps, cotton, trim
Decoupage, cyanotype,
fabric construction
3" x 16" x 10"

James Earl Ray, a confirmed racist and criminal, shot and killed Martin Luther King Jr. on April 4, 1968, in Memphis, Tennessee. On the following day, Robert F. Kennedy, the United States Senator from New York who was campaigning to earn the 1968 Democratic presidential nomination, addressed our country regarding the tragedy. The words of Robert F. Kennedy were inspiring:

"Our lives on this planet are too short and the work to be done too great to let this spirit flourish any longer in our land. But we can perhaps remember- even if only for a short time- that those who live with us are our brothers, that they share with us the same short movement of life, that they seek - as we do- nothing but the chance to live out their lives in purpose and happiness, winning what satisfaction and fulfillment they can.

"Surely this bond of common faith, this bond of common goal, can begin to teach us something. Surely we can learn, at least, to look at those around us as fellow men and surely we can begin to work a little harder to bind up the wounds among us and to become in our hearts brothers and countrymen once again."

What strides have we made since Robert F. Kennedy called for peace? Sadly, today remains a "time of shame and sorrow." When will it end?

OLLE JOHANSON
*People! This is trash.*
Brass, sterling and paper
Fabrication
9" x 8" x 6"

DEB TODD WHEELER
*Wartime Nutrition v.2*
3 minute video
projection with sound

I selected a modest and engraved gun as my starting point and was stunned by it's simplicity and elegance. A key part of the process was researching gun violence in my adopted state of New Mexico. The statistics on the numbers and frequency of gun deaths are appalling and underscore the untenable position of many of our politicians who block efforts to create real change in our laws. My gun is now the housing for an accordion book which tells a story about domestic violence in New Mexico and the toll it takes upon women and children. With the assistance of a screwdriver, the book can be folded and becomes part of the gun grip.

**JULIA M. BARELLO**
*In the State of New Mexico, Accordion Book*
Recycled gun, recycled MRI film
Laser cutter and hand fabrication
3¼" x 12" x 12"

750,000.

ROY
*Remembrance*
Cymbal, plaster, gun
Cold connections, sculpting
9" x 9" x 1"

This piece is a remembrance of the Greek, Christian genocide in what is now present day Turkey 94 years ago. The estimated death toll was 750,000 and that is the handwritten number on my wall sculpture. My grandfather crossed the same waters as the Syrian migrants today, risking everything, and landing on the Greek island of Chios.

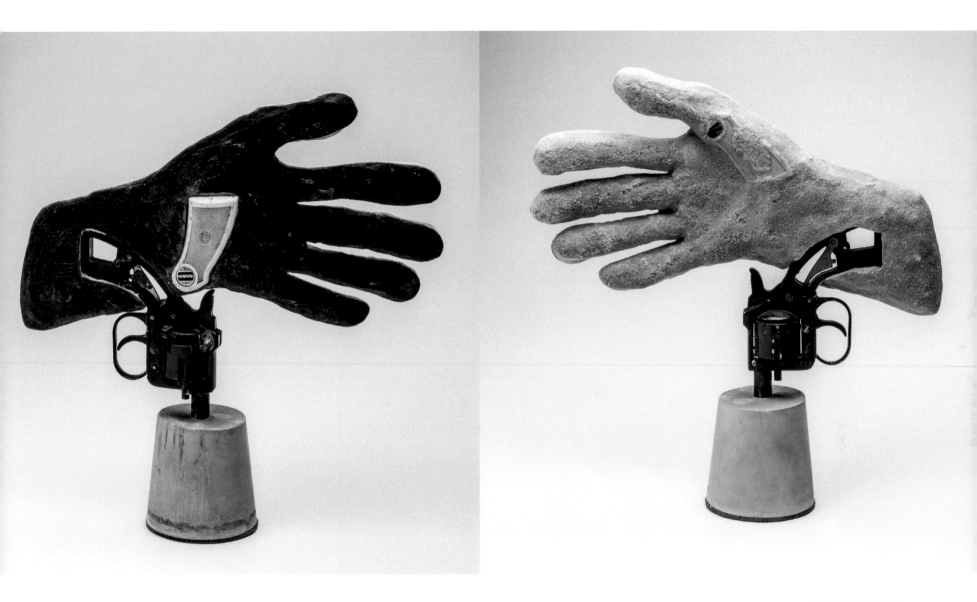

VALERIE MITCHELL
*Handshake*
Cement, steel pistol with plastic, stain, wax
Hand poured cement with object and
metal armature
11" x 10" x 3"
Photo: Ricardo Mendoza

DONALD A. STUART
*Still Waters*...........
Aluminum, brass, sterling silver,
mirrored Plexiglas, wood, paint, steel
Forging, welding, fabrication
11" x 12" x 7"

**GLEN S. GARDNER**
*Family Heirloom*
Handgun, 3d printed
metal, wood, velvet
Hand sculpted skull
model, digitally
scanned to create
digital model, 3d
printed via ExOne
Co. direct to metal
process, general
metalsmithing
techniques
13¼" x 15½" x 2"

HARRINGTON & RICHARDSON ARMS CO.
WORCESTER, MASS. U.S.A.
PAT. APRIL 2ND. 1896

Growing up in the 50's, cowboys were my heroes. My grandfather also shared this deep affection for everything concerning the Wild West. With his encouragement and mentoring, by the age of 12, I had learned to ride, and SHOOT. The crack and mule kick upon firing a 30-30 deer rifle at age 8 was a terrifying, but also an exhilarating experience. My grandfather was also something of a myth buster. So, at this tender age, I learned the difference between movie heroes and the true realities of firearms. For me, these lessons have never been forgotten. Regrettably, these lessons and harsh realities concerning this most lethal form of metalwork seem to be mostly ignored, or maybe, simply forgotten? The handgun I received for this project is over 100 years old. It most likely sat idle in a garage drawer for decades. It was probably passed from one generation to the next by someone's grandfather. While I marvel at its precision and fine engineering, I have no illusions about its terrible purpose. My entry, "Family Heirloom" takes the form of a memento. Drawing upon my childhood memories it offers a somewhat crazy mixture of honor, respect, terror and regret.

TONY ESOLA
*Adolescent Allure*
Cast iron, steel, enamel, gun
Cast, enameled, fabricated
9" x 4½" x 6"

**JESSICA CALDERWOOD**
*Pink Guns Blazing*
Porcelain, vitreous china, found shell casings, steel,
copper, milk paint, rubber
Slip casting, cold connections
8" x 6" x 6"

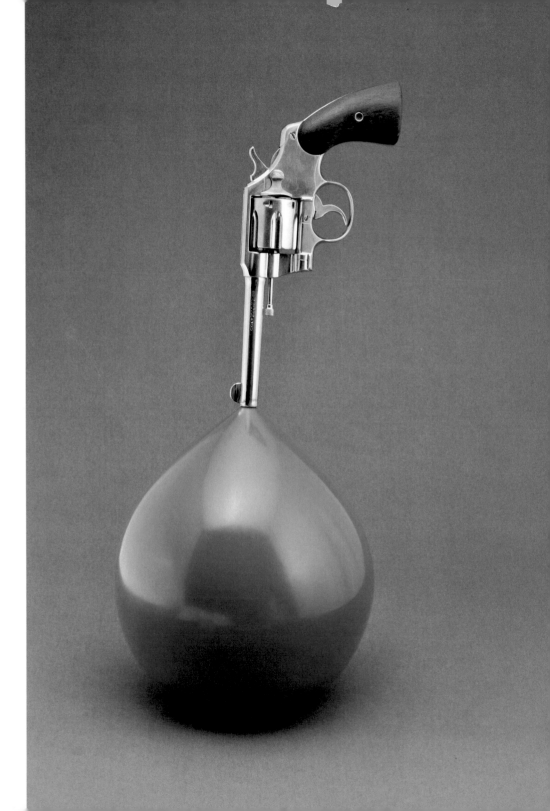

JOE MUENCH
*Bubble Gun*
Handgun, steel, wood, chrome, paint, plastic
The "bubble" form is hand formed and
fabricated using traditional metalsmithing and
automotive/aircraft metal shaping techniques.
TIG and torch welded, hand finished, painted
with enamel paint, threaded
19" x 12" x 10"

REBECCA STRZELEC
*Gubbles*
3D Printed ABS Plastic and gun grips
3D modeling, assembly
Tray: 1" x 9" x 9"
Orange Gubble: 3½" x 9¾" x 13"
Yellow Gubble: 3½" x 9" x 11"

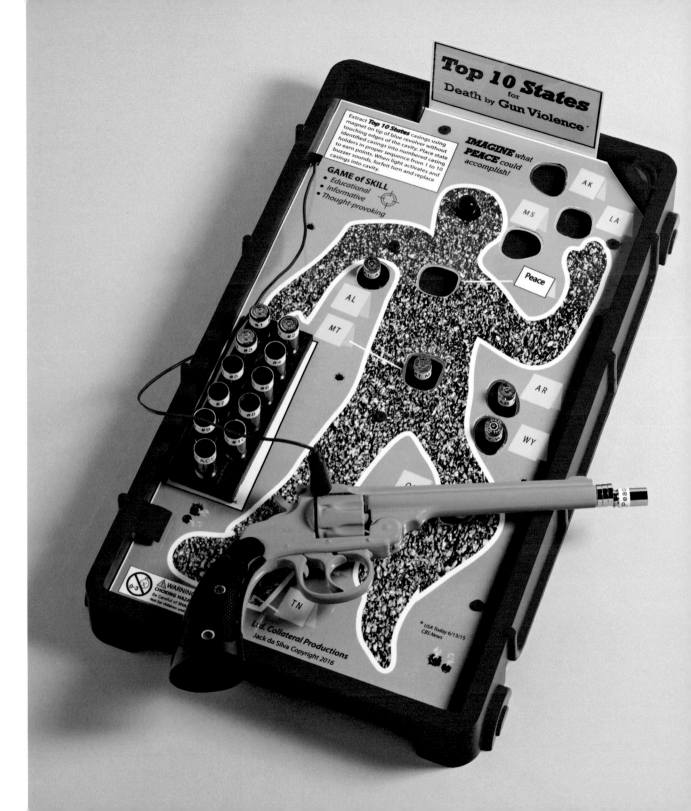

JACK da SILVA
*Top Ten States for Death by Gun Violence*
Electric game board, powder coated revolver,
shell casings, wood, laminated graphic game
board design, brass rod, magnet
Fabrication, assemblage, soldering, powder
coating, game board graphic design created
via Adobe Illustrator
7" x 9" x 16"
Photo: M. Lee Fatherree, Oakland, CA

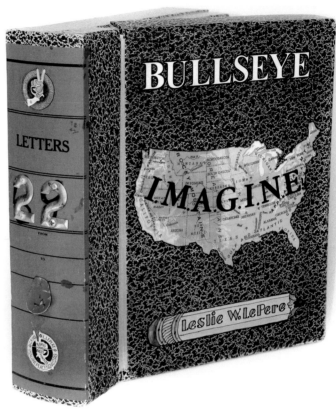

**LESLIE W. LePERE**
*Bullseye*
Paper, india ink, colored pencil,
plexiglass, found objects
Assemblage
13" x 11" x 3"
Photo: Gay Waldman

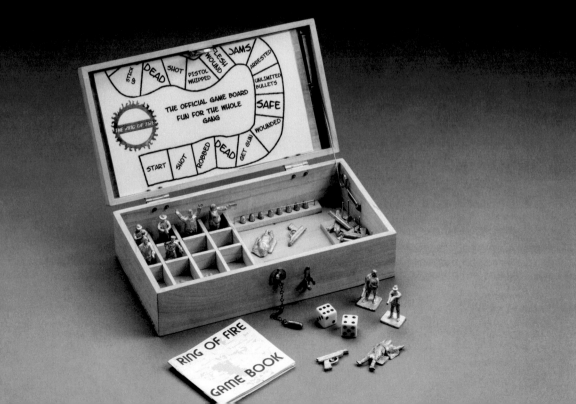

The Gun Control Act of 1968 was passed by Congress to stop the import of cheap handguns known as "Saturday Night Specials." Junk guns. These guns have no other use than to stickup convenience stores. The law did not prevent the manufacture nor sale of these guns domestically. Los Angeles became host to six companies that produced "SNS." They were Arcadia, Bryco Arms, Lorcin Engineering, Davis, Phoenix and Sundance Industries. Law enforcement referred to this area of LA as the "Ring of Fire."

The gun I received came from the "Ring of Fire." It was a Lorcin .380 CAL automatic, truly a piece of crap. The only steel parts in this gun are the barrel, several small parts and a couple of springs. The grips and trigger are plastic. The frame and slide are cast ZAMAK, a low temperature zinc alloy. The melted gun produced 1.04 lbs of ZAMAK for me to work with.

I was struck with the feeling of games being played between our government, gun companies, criminals and private citizens. Candy Land meets Clue gives us the Ring of Fire game. All game tokens are cast ZAMAK reclaimed from the Lorcin 380.

**CHRISTOPHER DARWAY**
*Ring of Fire*
ZAMAK zinc alloy, poplar wood,
brass, nu-gold bronze
Reclaimed ZAMAK alloy, lost wax
vacuum cast, fabrication
10" x 5½" x 3"

**CAITLIN SKELCEY**
*Hollow*
1898 Harrington & Richardson 32 revolver,
polyester resin, infiltrated gypsum powder,
automotive paint and Clearcoat.
Welding, painting, molding, 3D printing
8" x 9" x 5½"

JOSHUA DeMONTE
*Industry Product*
Gun, 33% glass-filled polyamide,
vinyl, acrylic, screws
CAD, digital fabrication, drawing
9" x 11" x 2½"

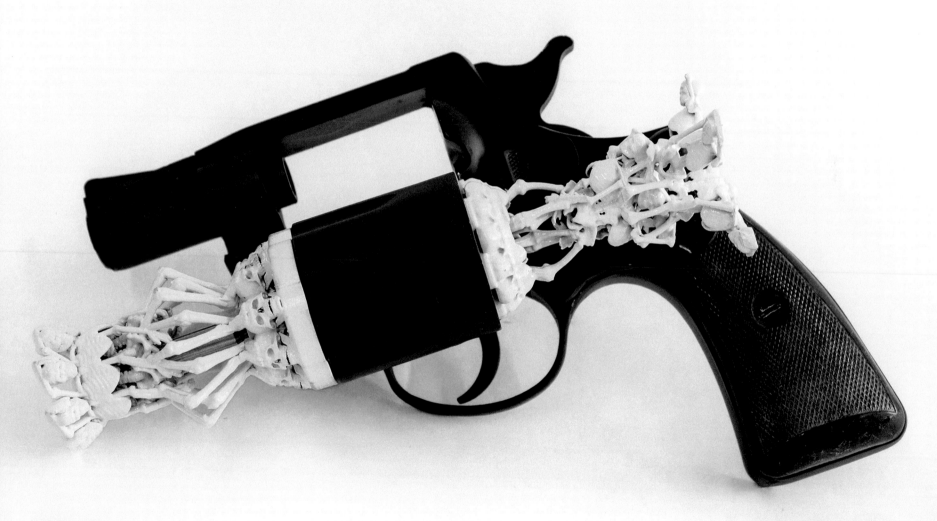

ARTHUR HASH
*The Not So Merry Go Round*
Sterling silver, resin and gun
CAD modeling, 3D printing and
lost wax casting
3" x 6" x 2½"

LIZ CLARK
*Projectile Disfunction*
Brass, copper, steel
Sawing, fabrication,
riveting crimping
4" x 10" x 2½"

SONYA CLARK
*Earthbound*
Thread, gun
Wrapping
6" x 4" x 2"
Photo: Taylor Dabney

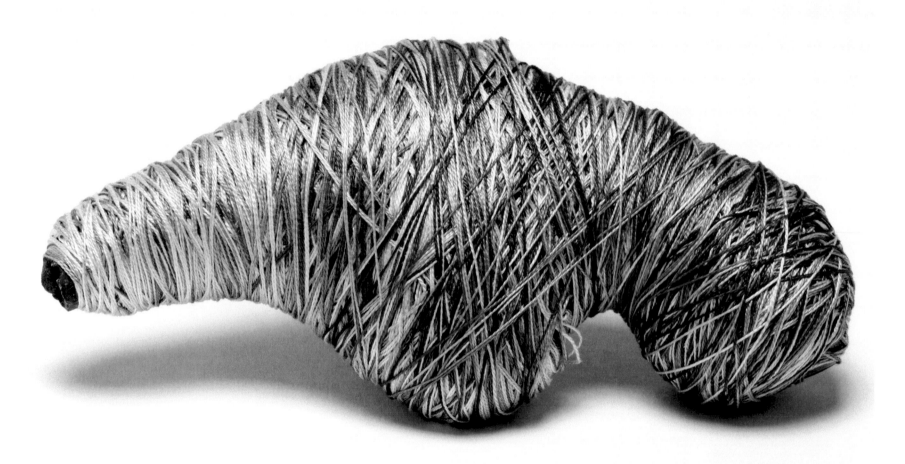

We smelt the metal from the earth, harness its malleability and shape it into a design that seems to yield power. But, that power is false. It only serves to bring our bodies back to the earth.

imagine war
guns shot by guns
domino chain

one gun remains
iron fisted
imagine peace

*anyhow*

JOHANNA DAHM
*Imagine War*
A gun shot with a gun
Shooting
9" x 6" x 1⁹/₁₆"

ROB MILLARD-MENDEZ
*Safe, Effective, Stylish Handgun Storage*
*Device for the Home*
Wood (walnut, ebony), steel, disabled handgun,
shell casings, cast concrete
The gun was cast into the house-shaped
concrete mold. Traditional dovetail joinery was
used to create the base of the project. The
ebony "bullets" were turned on a lathe and then
inserted into the metal bullet casings.
12" x 12" x 9"

SHARON MASSEY
*New Normal*
Enamel, resin inlay, 9mm
handgun
Cloisonne, etching, inlay
5" x 7" x 1"

# WHAT GUNS ARE GOOD FOR:

1. KILLING HIGH SCHOOL STUDENTS

2. KILLING COLLEGE STUDENTS & PROFESSORS

3. KILLING ELECTED OFFICIALS

4. KILLING ELEMENTARY SCHOOL STUDENTS & TEACHERS

5. KILLING UNARMED CITIZENS ANYWHERE

6. KILLING YOUR FAMILY

**7. KILLING YOURSELF**

THOMAS MANN
*The American (Double Action) Dream*
Clear plexiglass, digital prints, patterned
brass, copper, brass
Collage and assemblage
4" x 7" x ¾"

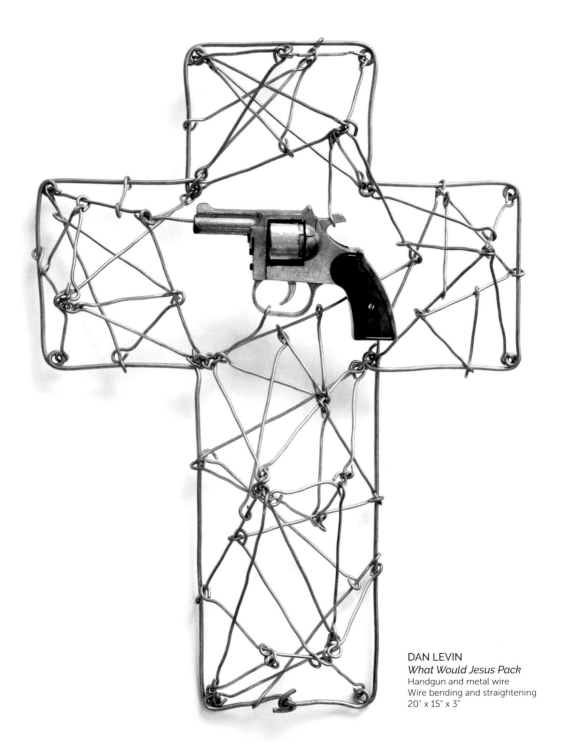

DAN LEVIN
*What Would Jesus Pack*
Handgun and metal wire
Wire bending and straightening
20" x 15" x 3"

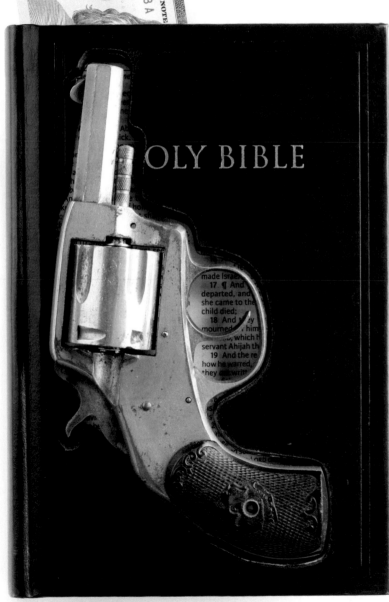

The first time I had a gun pulled on me I was at a Christmas party. I might have been 17 years old. I worked for these three brothers in Detroit and they had invited me to this party. After a few drinks and some joking around I made a mistake and cracked a rude joke regarding one of the brothers. His older brother immediately pulled a gun out and pointed it at my head, and the world fell away.

GERALD WECKESSER
*American Conversation*
Gun, Bible, wood, U.S. currency
Laser cutting, woodworking
9" x 7" x 2½"

MATTHEW HOLLERN
*Rest in Peace*
Pewter, bronze, nylon,
wood, paint, satin, gun
Pewter fabrication, casting,
3D modeling, SLS nylon
printing
19½" x 15" x 15"

**HEATH SATOW**
*Fetish*
Disabled guns, steel
Cutting, forming,
welding, grinding, gun
bluing, wax sealer
10½" x 9" x 6"

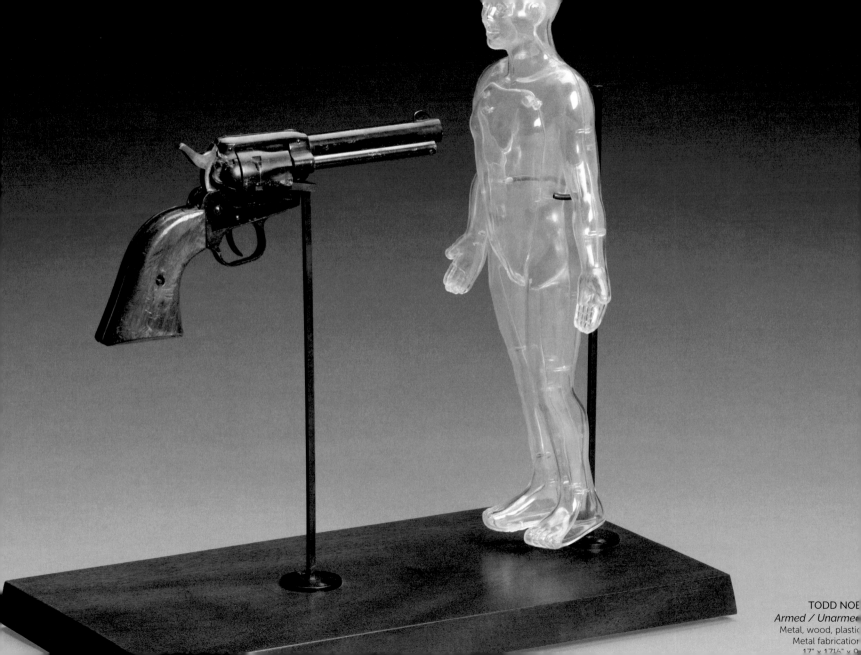

IF I COULD I'D CRACK A NUT OR TWO

JOYCE J. SCOTT
*Oh Say Can You See*
Modified metal gun, wooden nut
cracker, glass beads, thread, wire
Assemblage, peyote stitch
8" x 10" x 15"

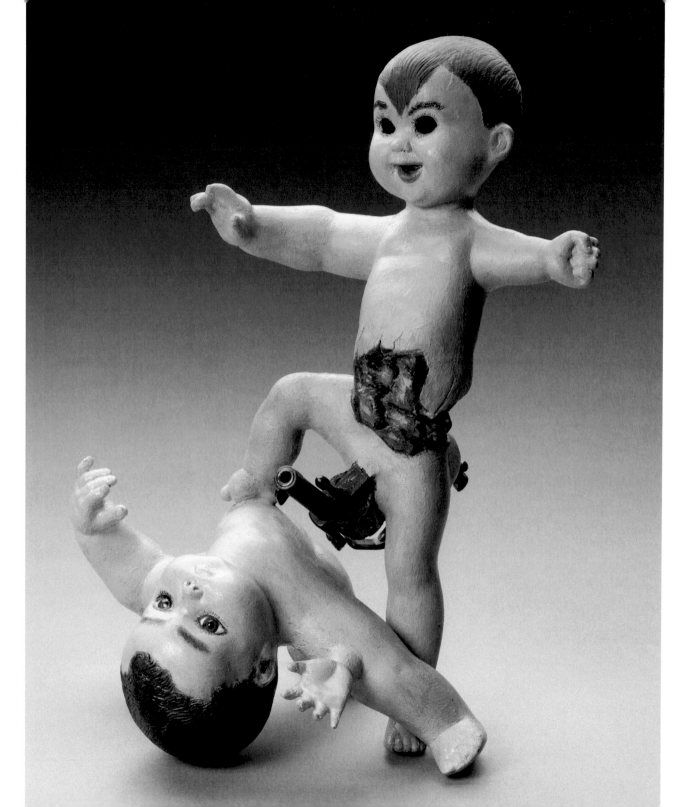

**SAMUEL SHAW**
*Cocked Gun*
Porcelain, gun, oil paint
Fabricated with
chemical bonds and
joining compounds
14" x 10" x 10"

RIES NIEMI
*Trophy Mount*
Gun, steel, velvet,
embroidery
Welded steel with computer
embroidery on velvet
9" x 7" x 2"

When I first received my revolver in the mail; I was shocked, that even with the knowledge that it had been rendered inoperable, how carefully and fearfully I responded to it. Before I had even opened the box I cautiously transported it to my studio as to not disturb it, and when working with it I was always careful not to ever have the barrel facing towards me. There was something about that gun, that even when rendered harmless created such anxiety and concern within me. For some reason I seemed to infer that it had a life of its own.

The imagery, terminology, and pop culture references which unite the penis to guns is well established. While I was planning this piece, I kept returning to my initial fear that my revolver had a mind of its own, and could erupt at any minute. That any object could act independent of the desires of its operator, felt akin to men's often used excuse of their 'little member' having a mind of its own and getting them into trouble sexually. To divorce responsibility from the operator of an object or organ, and displacing the blame felt like an interesting topic that I wanted to explore. With this piece and within the frame of 'gun as penis, penis as gun' I wanted to explore how personal responsibility could once again fully fall back solely upon the operator of these objects. Male chastity works by ensuring that the user cannot become sexually aroused while caged, and similarly I chose to display the revolver cradled facing the owner in the operators hands. Both objects are rendered inoperable by the owner, and are impossible to 'go off' without outside intervention.

ANDREW KUEBECK
*These Hands Are Not For Hurting:
Rendered Harmless*
Copper, enamel, felt, image on enamel,
found gun trigger, gold leaf
Electroformed, enameled, set, image
transfer onto glass
12" x 12" x 4"

TOM MUIR
*Penis Envy Prosthetic*
Steel, ABS plastic, brass, beeswax, powder
coat, Brownell's spray grit
3D digital modeling and printing, forging,
fabrication, powder-coating
6⅞" x 6¾" x 11⅜"
Photo: Tim Thayer

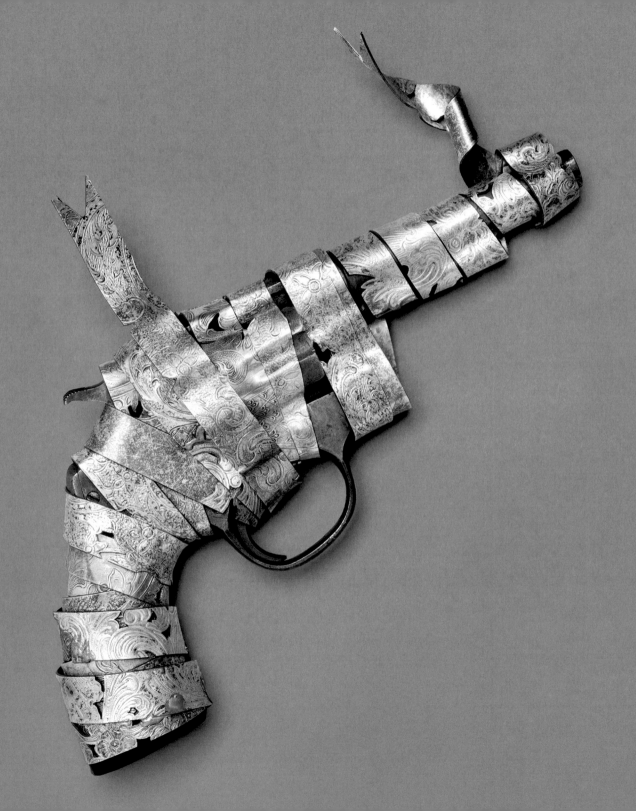

JAYDAN MOORE
*Weapon/We*
Silver-plated platters
Forming, soldering
12" x 7" x 2"

SHINGO FURUKAWA
*Untitled (a gun on a featherbed)*
Steel, aluminium, brass feathers, gun
Machining, welding, etc.
9" x 12" x 12"

man and gun
hand in hand
insane couple

**JOHANNA DAHM & JOHANNA STIERLIN**
*Hand in Hand*
Disabled SIG P 210 pistol
Moulage: wax, paint, human hair
8" x 5⅛" x 1³⁄₁₆"
Photo: Reinhard Zimmermann

PHIL RENATO
*Irreverensibility*
Nylon, polyurethane paint
3D scanning, 3D fluid dynamic modeling,
Selective Laser Sintered 3D printing,
automotive airbrushing
5" x 5½" x 14"

RIMAS VisGIRDA
*Guns R Us*
Porcelain, underglazes, glaze,
revolver, paint, PC-7, French cleat
Make slab, decorate slab, fire slab,
attach gun, attach French cleat
9⅝" x 13¾" x 1¾"

MELISSA DAVENPORT
*The Fixer*
Steel, brass, plastic, found objects
Sawing, filing, welding
5" x 8" x 2"

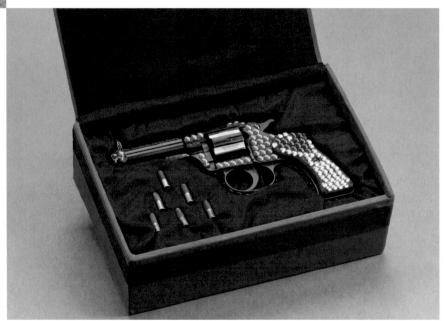

Thinking of You . . . Thinking of You . . . the people whose futures were cut short by the momentary firing of a gun. Thinking of You . . . the victims of domestic disputes, accidental discharge, hate crimes, mass shootings, gang violence, ideological fervor, suicide, armed robbery, law enforcement aggression and just being in the wrong place at the wrong time. Thinking of You . . . a colorful, flowered balloon exploding from a fire arm printed with a saying that we use when we care, but don't know what to do. Thinking of You . . . bowing your head in silent mourning as our elected officials refuse to listen to our demands for gun law reform . . . the people whose futures were cut short by the momentary firing of a gun. Thinking of You . . . the victims of domestic disputes, accidental discharge, hate crimes, mass shootings, gang violence, ideological fervor, suicide, armed robbery, law enforcement aggression and just being in the wrong place at the wrong time. Thinking of You . . . a colorful, flowered balloon exploding from a fire arm printed with a saying that we use when we care, but don't know what to do. Thinking of You . . . bowing your head in silent mourning as our elected officials refuse to listen to our demands for gun law reform.

LINDA HESH & ERIC MARGRY
*Thinking of You*
Disabled gun, mylar balloon, acrylic, billboard media, brass, fiberfill, steel, chemical bonding
Assembled
16" x 20" x 3"

**LONEY METAL WORKS
ANNA LONEY & DON BELL**
*American Maelstrom*
Steel, copper wire, disabled
handgun
Fabrication
12" x 16" x 11"

**JIM COTTER**
*The Smoking Gun*
Cement, gun, cigarettes,
wood, glass, cadel
Cement casting &
staging
11" x 9" x 17"

**LESLIE A. GOLOMB**
*My Little Unicorn*
Metal, yarn, and stuffed animal
Wrapping
8" x 10" x 3"

**LEO SEWELL**
*Disarmed: The 32 Caliber Collection*
Reclaimed objects
Assemblage
13" x 11" x 2"

# JUROR STATEMENTS

# JUROR STATEMENTS

**Boris Bally**

Metalsmith

"Do we not have
the power to
transcend these
threatening objects
by transforming them
beyond their deadly
utilitarian design?
Can't art diffuse
violence?"

## LOADED ART

Since my 1994 affiliation with the Pittsburgh Anti-Violence Coalition, I have applied my craft skills to reconfiguring guns from government buy-back programs into artwork that advocates for non-violence. And, in recent years, as gun violence has escalated, my interest has intensified.

While in Denver to speak at the 2012 Colorado Metalsmithing Association conference, I was stunned to learn that a shooter had just terrorized an Aurora theater complex close to our hotel. In a matter of minutes, the young man had killed 12 and wound 70 others. He was armed with several legally obtained firearms after background checks were performed.[1] The tragic massacre, so close at hand, has haunted me since.

Just two months after the Aurora massacre, the United States was devastated by the Sandy Hook shooting, which took 26 lives, 20 of them children's. In the subsequent years, waves of gun violence swept Rosebud, Oregon; Charlestown, South Carolina; Waco, Texas; Orlando, Florida; and many more.

In 2015 alone, there were 332 confirmed mass shootings in the U.S.[2] Based on gun homicide statistics published by the American Journal of Medicine, we live in the most dangerous developed country in the world.[3] I've become preoccupied with the sorrow brought on by gun violence at the hands of people who should not have had access to weapons. My question: Is there no way to monitor, regulate, and enforce who gets to have a gun and who does not?

And why does any citizen need an assault rifle? We have laws against drinking while driving and are required to wear seatbelts. We regulate tobacco because the evidence shows it kills us. We aren't allowed to carry bombs into public buildings. Clearly, access to guns is an urgent public health and safety priority. Why can't our society address this scourge and revise our laws to protect us?

Other nations do much better. Just 12 days after the 1996 Port Arthur massacre in Southern Tasmania, Australia radically reformed its gun laws and initiated a national buy-back. There have been no mass shootings there since. None.

The month before I arrived to speak at the January 2016 East Carolina University art department's symposium "Materials Topics: In Flux," 14 people were shot and killed in San Bernardino, California.

Enough already!

What power do we have as artists to bring about positive change in society? That question prompted my decision, given the rise in gun violence, to get more involved and step up my own efforts to forge solutions. Contemplating the rebirth of the original 1997 "Artists of a Different Caliber" show, I conferred with my metalsmith colleagues at the ECU symposium. Their overwhelming support and promise to participate gave me the confidence to initiate this project and make it a reality. Since then, I became determined to succeed by any possible means. Building a community of like-minded artists, we seized this opportunity to bring these critical issues to the forefront.

Metalsmiths are intrigued by material, techniques, and construction challenges. It is poignant that we rely on hands to guide our tools, shaping the objects we dream up for adornment, play, exploration and utility. We strive to communicate through layers of

deeper meaning. Unfortunately, some of our designs become dangerous contraptions – weapons such as knives and pistols. They may be created to be ornamental, of course, but also to defend, to threaten, and, too often, to kill.

Hands make pistols. Pistols fit ergonomically into hands. We respect the handcraft that goes into making the weapon as an object. Do we not have the power to transcend these threatening objects by transforming them beyond their deadly utilitarian design? Can't art diffuse violence?

How symbolic it is that, just a year after the ECU symposium, this exhibition will make its debut at the ECU campus to become part of the next symposium's programming. May this catalogue facilitate dialogue, action, and positive change.

1    CBS News, "Colo. shooter purchased guns legally from 3 different stores," By Michelle Castillo, July 20, 2012, 7:38 PM
2    http://www.gunviolencearchive.org
3    CBS News, "How U.S. gun deaths compare to other countries," By Robert Preidt Healthday, February 3, 2016, 1:44 PM

*Boris Bally / "Loaded Menorah"*

Instead of the heavy bullet belts identifying G.I.s and Bandits, we created an alternate wearable artwork made of dissected rifle barrels tucked into a soft white sash. The wearer feels the immense weight of these formerly powerful weapons, now rendered inoperable. This decorative tube belt becomes more powerful than bullets, which require rifles in order to fly. The white ribbon, unstained by blood, symbolizes peace and tranquility. The red stitching reminds us of the blood that has already spilled.

**IRENE LaVON WALKER & BORIS BALLY**
*ROR: Release on Recognizance
(Rosary of Rounds)*
Hand-woven cloth, elastic, silver .925, 242 steel barrels cut from over 43 disabled rifles, shotguns and pistols
Hand-woven, hand fabricated and machined
116½" x 3¾" x 2
Photo: Tillett Studios
Model: Jennifer Bruyneel

# JUROR STATEMENTS

**Monica Moses**

Editor in Chief

American Craft Magazine

"Art is not a magic bullet. (Pun intended.) But art changes the world, Jerry Saltz says, "incrementally and by osmosis." We must do more."

## GUNS, THE AMERICAN INFATUATION

Artists show us the familiar in fresh terms. They open our eyes. They enable learning. In "I.M.A.G.I.N.E Peace Now," 101 artists show us guns in new ways. And if there's a device in American life that needs to be understood anew, examined from different angles, it's the gun.

Firearms are deeply rooted in the American identity – at least in the identity we associate with males of European extraction who arrived here two or three hundred years ago. Our cultural heritage and our history books are replete with stories of frontiersmen slashing through wilderness, guns at their sides, ready to defend against bears, cougars, rattlesnakes, and – it needs to be said – Native Americans.

In the mainline American story, guns have long had a visceral, patriotic importance, alongside the flag, the military, and the national anthem. They've represented resourcefulness, self-determination, a path through a dangerous, strange, new land. In a sense, guns made America possible. Guns were tools of triumph.

Today, of course, guns have other meanings. They're more prevalent, more sophisticated, more deadly. As Rob Jackson points out in the artist statement for "Single Shot", when the Second Amendment was written, guns needed to be reloaded after one shot was fired. Today's popular semi-automatic rifles fire hundreds of rounds per minute.

We're a long way from the frontier. Today, guns are used more impulsively, more recklessly. They're used every day, many times a day, to kill people. In 2015 alone, more than 32,000 Americans were killed by guns. In that awful number are suicides, domestic violence deaths, children caught in gang cross-fire, and that horrifying staple of 21st-century American life – the mass shooting on campuses and in workplaces. Even in churches, for God's sake.

The "I.M.A.G.I.N.E" artists took fresh aim at the old gun mystique. Biba Schutz's "Another Day" makes a straightforward case. Attached to a 22-caliber revolver is a cotton flag embroidered with the essential, grisly facts. On an average day in 2015, 297 people were shot in the United States – 89 killed, 53 of which were suicides. During the year, there were 372 mass shootings, each involving four or more victims. You can't look at "Another Day" and romanticize guns; you're too busy calculating the bloodshed.

Rebecca Strzelec and Leeann Herreid took a different direction: disarmament. Strzelec's "Gubble" and Herreid's "Squash Blossom Necklace" reimagine the familiar form of a gun grip as part of a child's toy and a charming piece of jewelry. Imagine our weapons transformed and used for good, these pieces say.

Tom Muir, Gerald Weckesser, and Dan Levin point to the bizarre intertwining of gun culture, hyper-masculinity, business, and religion. In Muir's "Penis Envy Prosthetic", a hot pink plastic penis forms the barrel of a gun; the grip is a matching scrotum. A revolver fits snugly into a Bible bookmarked by a $100 bill in Weckesser's "American Conversation". In Levin's "What Would Jesus Pack", a revolver forms the center of a crude wire cross. The gun-toting, Bible-quoting crusader for "liberty" and the traditional, male-dominated family is familiar to Americans. These pieces reveal just how grotesque that figure is.

What are guns good for? That's the question Tom Mann poses in his devastating piece. He lists seven things, starting with "killing high school students" and ending with "killing yourself." The focal point of the piece, the barrel of a gun, has been replaced by an image of a man with a gun pointed at his temple. I knew a guy who, while negotiating a pizza order with his wife, picked up a gun on the kitchen counter and blew his brains out. We all have these stories. That's what happens when life is stressful and the tools of death are within arm's reach.

Whatever the value of guns to the European settlers we revere in our history, they represent something else today: Guns are sickening instruments of terror and destruction. As artifacts of Americana, they are costing us. No – literally – they are killing us. In droves. It's imperative that we stem the bloody tide, that we unlearn our love of guns.

Exhibitions such as "I.M.A.G.I.N.E." help us envision a new kind of America, wary of weapons and committed to the peaceful resolution of conflict. If political change comes, it will most likely germinate in our culture. And artists can lead the way. Smoking declined after people saw a Marlboro-Man-type figure coughing uncontrollably in public service announcements. A remarkably swift acceptance of gay rights followed Will & Grace and La Cage aux Folles.

Art is not a magic bullet. (Pun intended.) But art changes the world, Jerry Saltz says, "incrementally and by osmosis." We must do more.

**Shepard Fairey**

Artist, Designer & Activist

Obey Giant

"When I ponder the demand for these killing machines, I see Satan metaphorically at work in the darkest, fear-based impulses of humanity. We can rise above and be better!"

## GOD SAVES AND SATAN INVESTS

*The following excerpt is the inspiration behind Shepard's "God Saves and Satan Invests" print and can also be found on his website, www.obeygiant.com.*

I'm not a big fan of the absurd abundance of guns in the U.S. I'm also perplexed by the claim of much of the nation to have "Christian values". If god tells us to love our neighbor and not to take another human life, where do the assault weapons and piles of ammo fit into these "Christian values"? I personally think assault weapons fall more in the "Satan's values" category. Anyway, if you claim to dig god, lay off of satan's tools. If you don't believe in god, lay off of satan's tools! We live in statistically the safest time in human history, so the idea one would need an assault weapon for self defense is ridiculous. These weapons are tools of aggression, not defense, and any sane person not clouded by irrational fear would reach the same conclusion. When I ponder the demand for these killing machines, I see Satan metaphorically at work in the darkest, fear-based impulses of humanity. We can rise above and be better!

I get the 2nd Amendment, but the right to bear arms should NOT BE UNCONDITIONAL.

The 2nd Amendment reads:

"A well regulated Militia, being necessary to the security of a free State, the right of the people to keep and bear Arms, shall not be infringed." It was adopted in 1791 shortly after the Revolutionary War in which the colonies had freed themselves from an English monarchy that gave the colonies no representation. The wisdom of the 2nd Amendment was to ensure that a state militia could combat dictatorial oppression. I would assert that putting guns in the hands of a large portion of the civilian population was probably not what the founding fathers had in mind. I'd also say that our nations founders could not have predicted the rise of technology enabling people to acquire weapons capable of shooting dozens of rounds in mere seconds. My concern over very easy access to guns seems reasonably well founded. I'm perplexed by America's love of guns. I grew up in South Carolina hunting with my dad and we always had shotguns in the house. My dad put a framed piece in my room that said "A wise hunter once said: all the Pheasants ever bred won't repay for one man dead". I was taught to honor and value human life. Also, the shotguns used for hunting were required by law for duck hunting, to only hold three shells at a time. The idea was that it was excessive to shoot more than three times at a bird. No one needs a gun that shoots 10, 20, 50 rounds. Whatever your feelings are about hunting, you can use a three shot shotgun to defend your home, but guns are easy to misuse. A lot of people claim to own guns for self-defense, but check out the statistics below. Guns lead to intentional or unintentional misuse far more often than they are used for justifiable, self-defense related homicides. The Self Defense stats for every time a gun in the home is used in a self-defense homicide, a gun will be used in:

- 1.3 accidental deaths
- 4.6 criminal homicides
- 37 suicides

Let's save lives and hold lawmakers and the NRA accountable! Thanks for caring.

Art courtesy Shepard Fairey / ObeyGiant.com

"Duality of Humanity I" (l), "God Saves and Satan Invests" (r)

## DEDICATION

Arien D. Daly

April 17, 1983 - August 22, 2015

Arien's sunny life was tragically cut short when she was murdered by an ex-boyfriend who then turned the gun on himself.

ACKNOWLEDGEMENTS

# CATALOG & EXHIBITION SUPPORT

## CATALOG SUPPORT:

### $1000+ Gold Sponsor
Bally Family (Zollikon, Switzerland)
Kurt Coppo
Johanna Dahm
Enamel Arts Foundation
Christine Huber
Donna McMillan
Andrew Ory
The Society of Arts and Crafts, Boston
Michael Staenberg

### $500+ Silver Sponsor
Robert Ebendorf
Ciril & Kylee Hitz
Matthew Hollern & Pamela Argentieri
Ken & Sandra Lambert
Leslie LePere
Barbara McFadyen
Coleen & Howard Witt Messing
Chris Rifkin
Sueños, Arlette & Kaspar Rüegg
Aaron & Lynn Usher
Bryan Vansell

## CATALOG SUPPORT (cont.):

### $250+ Bronze Sponsor
Andrea Arena
Alex & Doris Bally
Dominique Bereiter
Gary Cohen
Ellen-Deane Cummins
Marilyn da Silva
Alyda Dewhirst
Will Fairbrother
Rachelle R. Green
Marty Kaplan
Peter Karczmar & Cathy Lund
Charlie King
Joanne Lang
Meaulnes Legler
Jim Lesko
Carol Maione
Michael McMillan
John Rais
The Saneholtz Family
Stephen Saracino
Brett Smiley & Jim DeRentis

## JURY AWARDS SUPPORT:

### 1st Place Gold:
Susan Bucknam Award - $1000

### 2nd Place Silver:
E.H. Schwab Award - $500

### 3rd Place Bronze:
Halstead Award - $300

### Honorable Mentions:
Munya Avigail Upin Award
Honorable Mention - $150

Halstead Award
Honorable Mention - $150

Doug White Award
Honorable Mention - $150

Stephen Saracino Award
Honorable Mention - $150

Kendall College of Art & Design Award
Honorable Mention - $150

CRAFTHAUS Award
Honorable Mention - $150

## EXHIBITION SUPPORT:

Artists participating in the show donated their valuable time, creative energy and also the seed money to launch this show.

### $1000+
ALCHEMY 9•2•5
Anonymous

### $250+
Kendall College of Art & Design

### $100+
Theresa Lovering Brown
Carla Martine
Stephen Saracino
Jay Sprague for 'Emma'
Several Anonymous Donors

# ADDITIONAL SUPPORT

# WITH SPECIAL THANKS

## KICKSTARTER $100+ STAKEHOLDER SPONSORS:

Dauvit Alexander
Daniel Anderson
Hilary Anderson
Patricia Appleby
Meg Auth
Marc Bally
Nico Bally
Jerry A. Belair
Gary & Sarah Blythe
Caro-Gray Bosca
Laura & Howard Brightman
Autumn Brown
Gail M. Brown
Kathleen Browne
Dana Cassara
Larry T. Christy
Christine Clark
Stephen Cohan
Lori Colina-Lee
Sheridan Conrad
Jim Cotter
Cappy Counard
Tim Cunningham
David Damkoehler
Chris Darway
Jack da Silva
Erica & David DeMarco
Kirsten Denbow
Ivy Derderian
Sean Duffy
Joost During
Cynthia Eid
Tony Esola
Jeannine Falino
Teresa F Faris
Fabio Fernandez
Maureen Friend
Shingo Furukawa

Sheila Gaddie
Paul Gaudio
John Stuart Gordon
Derek Graham
Stacey Gross
Elaine Gunnell
Hoss Haley
Philip Hawthorne
Audrey Holland
Paul Housberg
Catherine Jacobi
Reena Kazmann
Anne Killeen
Robin Kraft
Lexie Kupers
Barbara Larsen
Timothy Lazure
Larry Leahy
Peter B Lewis
Billie Lim
Dan Loewenstein
Kris Lonergan
Jan Loney
Ana Lopez
Ellen Malnerich
Paul McClure
Rob Millard-Mendez
Valerie Mitchell
Maria Modlin
Moms Demand Action | RI
Michael W. Monroe
Sydney Montstream-Quas
Nancy Morgan
Thomas Muir
Dawn Nakanishi
Jennifer Komar Olivarez
Ali Palaia
Patina Gallery

Sara Picard
Marissa Picheria
Chris Ploof
Ron Porter
Jennifer Ramirez
Margaret Ratliff
Dindy Reich
Phil Renato
Bryan Rinebolt
Tom Robbins
Anouk Savineau
Gerard Savineau
Linda Savineau
Sawing Machine
Kiki Sciullo
Short & Karl Family
Elizabeth Shypertt
Mara Holt Skov
Dr. Peter J. Snyder
Elaine Sokoloff
Jay Sprague
Kayla Staigvil
Donald A Stuart
Judith & Arnold Taylor
Cassandra Thayer
Billie Theide
Susan Thornton
James Thurman
Marlene True
Corinna Vigier
Carol Warner
Stacey Lee Webber
Doug White
Wendy Woldenberg
Nancy Worden
Rochelle Yankwitt
Stephen Yusko
Rosanne Zimmerman

**Thank you to all the other contributors who were part of the almost 350 backers.**

Erin McManus, Book Design & Layout
Keith McManus, Video Production
Brett Reilly, Zeus Web Design
Aaron and Lynn Usher, Photography
Karl Treen, Advisor
Luiza DeCamargo
Fabio Fernandez
Robert Ebendorf
Les W. LePere
Sandy Parr's Charlie King
Hannah Zane Hines, Intern
Brijette Marie Stamp, Intern

### Jurors:

Emily Zilber, Boston Museum of Fine Arts, Contemp Decorative Arts
Monica Moses, Editor in Chief, American Craft Magazine
Shepard Fairey, Artist, Designer and Activist
Boris Bally, Metalsmith

### Writers:

Michael McMillan, Associate Curator, Fuller Craft Museum
Ian Alden Russel, Curator, Brown University's David Winton Bell Gallery
Jillian Moore, Metals Artist and Art Critic

# NOTES

NOTES

# NOTES